OCCASIONAL CONTRIBUTIONS FROM THE MUSEUM OF ANTHROPOLOGY OF THE UNIVERSITY OF MICHIGAN

No. 12

A STUDY OF THE GLACIAL KAME CULTURE

IN MICHIGAN, OHIO, AND INDIANA

BY

WILBUR M. CUNNINGHAM

WITH AN APPENDIX BY

JAMES B. GRIFFIN

ANN ARBOR

UNIVERSITY OF MICHIGAN PRESS

1948

ISBN (print): 978-1-949098-52-5
ISBN (ebook): 978-1-951538-51-4

Browse all of our books at
sites.lsa.umich.edu/archaeology-books.

Order our books from the University of Michigan
Press at www.press.umich.edu.

For permissions, questions, or manuscript queries,
contact Museum publications by email at umma-
pubs@umich.edu or visit the Museum website at
lsa.umich.edu/ummaa.

PREFACE

In 1940 Mr. Wilbur M. Cunningham, of Benton Harbor, Michigan, visited the Museum of Anthropology and brought with him considerable information on the Glacial Kame culture, particularly on the finds from the Burch site in Berrien County, Michigan. It was his desire to have this data published as an *Occasional Contribution*. Dr. Carl E. Guthe, at that time Director of the Museum of Anthropology, suggested that I might edit the manuscript prepared by Mr. Cunningham and prepare a short statement on the affiliations of the Glacial Kame culture.

In October, 1941, Cunningham's preliminary manuscript was received. In March, 1942, he read a condensed version before the Anthropology Section of the Michigan Academy of Science, Arts, and Letters. By January, 1943, the manuscript was returned to Cunningham with suggested revisions and the Appendix by James B. Griffin. In February, the manuscript was turned over to Dr. Guthe for publication. A series of circumstances followed which postponed publication by the Museum of Anthropology. In the fall of 1945 the manuscript was submitted to and accepted by *American Antiquity*. Again publication was postponed, and in 1947, as Director of the Museum of Anthropology, I accepted the publication for the *Occasional Contribution* series.

The paper by Mr. Cunningham was prepared in 1941 and 1943 and has not been subsequently revised. The Appendix on the cultural affiliations was prepared during 1942 and has not been revised or altered. It should be emphasized that the allocation of the Glacial Kame complex to any particular time period is uncertain. My interpretation is that it is relatively late within the Middle Woodland; Richard G. Morgan, of the Ohio State Museum, and George I. Quimby, of the Chicago Natural History Museum, believe that it belongs in the Early Woodland (Adena) horizon.

The Museum of Anthropology is indebted to Mr. Cunningham for submitting this manuscript for publication and for his patience during the vexing delays and disappointments which prevented its publication. We are also indebted to a great many individuals who contributed their time and effort. Their aid has been acknowledged in the body of the report and in the plate descriptions.

JAMES B. GRIFFIN

CONTENTS

ILLUSTRATIONS

PLATES

(Plates I–XI follow page 51.)

MAP

INTRODUCTION

THIS study was begun with the idea of obtaining and preserving such information as it was possible to gather regarding the discovery of the group of shell and copper artifacts described herein. My interest grew as I read the references and discovered how little had been written on this subject. I concluded that it might be of interest to others if the following information was collected in an effort to group as many facts as possible concerning this type of burial and the associated artifacts.

Much additional information might be brought to light by experienced archaeologists. I would appreciate additional information concerning other gravel burials or similar shell artifacts.

More than thirty-eight years ago, Warren K. Moorehead advanced the theory that a "Glacial Kame" culture existed.[1] In the earliest statements about it there was little or no attempt to list the attributes which composed this division of Ohio archaeological units. Later, however, Moorehead stated somewhat more definitely his views regarding this "culture":

> The third culture, and the one to which no one save the writer seems to have given much thought, is that of the Glacial Kame. Often, when traveling about the state in the past years, his attention has been called by farmers to gravel-pits in which human skeletons had been found. As all observers know, bones deposited in gravel are preserved almost indefinitely. Investigation of many such burials, and the history of others, bring to light interesting facts. Tubular pipes, cannel-coal ornaments, long, slender unio-shell gorgets, tubes of slate, and hematite plummets abound. . . . .
>
> Although the tribe that buried in the Glacial Kames is classed by the writer as distinct from the other two cultures (Fort Ancient and Hopewell) yet it is possible (although perhaps not probable) that these people may later have become the carriers of the Fort Ancient culture.[2]

[1] Moorehead, 1897, p. 261; 1899, p. 168.

[2] Moorehead, 1909, pp. 141–42.

Moorehead suggested that the Glacial Kame culture was early and constituted a separate group; Shetrone took the position that "these burials appear to pertain to any or all of the several cultures of the state, thus indicating that this form of interment cannot be taken as a trait peculiar to any one, but rather as a practice so natural as to be common to all."[3] In a later publication Shetrone did not discuss the Glacial Kame burials,[4] and apparently no concerted action has been taken to study the artifacts from such burials nor to determine whether or not they represent a distinct culture. On account of a lack of interest, or because of insufficient time and funds, little is known regarding this type of burial, which now presents a very definite problem.

It is realized that more evidence is necessary before attempting to classify accurately the traits represented by the deep gravel burials or to be certain of the age of this complex. As a result, I have hesitated to do much more than gather the evidence. A few of the traits characterized by this complex are in the so-called "Red Ochre Phase," a few in the Adena and in the Hopewellian. Later, when more facts are available, it may be determined to be a comparatively old manifestation of the Woodland group, but at present it would seem to have some traits not included in either the Red Ochre, Adena, or Hopewell.

THE BURCH SITE

During the year 1905 or 1906, Clark Burch, a farmer, while digging gravel to fill low spots in his barnyard, unearthed five human skeletons on his farm near Coldwater in Township 6 South, Range 7 West, Branch County, Michigan, less than twenty miles from the state line of Indiana. These skeletons were in a gravel deposit defined as glacial outwash and probably the remnant of a strong sandbar.[5] This glacial deposit is in the

[3] Shetrone, 1920, p. 164.

[4] Shetrone, 1931.

[5] Personal communication, R. A. Smith, Michigan state geologist. Leverett and Taylor, 1915, pp. 146–49.

middle of a marsh, which at one time was connected with a river system, and the skeletons were at an elevation of about nine feet above the level of the marsh. The gravel deposit was originally almost round, about 150 feet in diameter, and of an estimated average height of fifteen feet above the level of the marsh, the eastern part being somewhat higher than the other parts of the deposit. As far as can be estimated from a view of the premises, the deposit is about the same height as the land surrounding the marshy area. Two similar gravel deposits near by have never been explored.

No information can be obtained as to whether the burials were made in pits dug in the gravel or were made on the surface with gravel from another part of the deposit heaped over them. The circumstances surrounding the finding of these skeletons must be constantly kept in mind, and then it will be understood why definite statements cannot be made regarding many details.

The skeletons were taken to the farmyard where they were examined, photographed, and measured by a physician who has long since died and whose records cannot now be located. They were then placed in a corncrib and, with the exception of two skulls, one of which was loaned to a student of dentistry, were destroyed when that building later burned.

The physician who measured the bones is said to have made the statement that two of the skeletons were of unusually large persons. The photographer was interviewed, and although he distinctly remembered taking the pictures, he stated that the plates had been destroyed many years ago, and as far as he knew none of the photographs were in existence. One skull, (Pl. XI) with the lower jaw missing, has been obtained from the person to whom it was loaned.[6]

[6] Georg K. Neumann, of the Department of Anthropology, Indiana University, has been kind enough to make an examination of the skull, and his report and observations follow:

"*Description of the skull:* The calvarium is that of a male about forty years of age at death. It is undeformed, of medium weight, with sexual characteristics fairly well marked. The bone is in excellent state of preservation and seems to have retained a considerable amount of organic matter. The brain

Clark Burch, the finder of the skeletons, is still living on the same farm, and his testimony indicates that the burials were undoubtedly in a sitting position (flexed) with most of the artifacts "in their laps." With or near the skeletons he found much red paint, charcoal, some pieces two feet long, and many shell disk beads; the beads were so numerous that he and his helpers did not bother to pick up all of them. The bones were

---

case is ovoid. Brow ridges are about medium large and divided, the glabella small, the slope of the frontal medium, the frontal eminences poorly developed, and the forehead narrow. The parietal eminences are mediumly developed, the occipital region medium curved, and there is little if any lamdoidal flattening. The elevation of the occipital condyles and basion is medium. The orbits are oblong with little inclination; there is no suborbital fossa, giving a flat appearance to the face. The cheek bones are medium in size and medium in anterior and lateral projection. The nasion depression is small, the nasal root medium high and narrow, the bridge probably medium. The lower jaw is missing.

"The more important measurements are the following: Greatest length, 181; width, 142; basion-bregma height, 135; ear height, 111; least breadth of forehead, 96; total facial angle, 86°; bizygomatic width (across cheek bones), 140; upper facial height, 73; cranial capacity, 1380 cc.; basion-nasion length, 101; nasal height, 52; nasal width, 26; orbital height, 32; orbital width from maxillofrontale, 44; from dacryon, 41; and the interorbital breadth from maxillofrontale, 18. All measurements except angles and capacity are in millimeters.

"The more important indices are: Cranial 78.45 or mesocranial, height-length 74.59 or orthocranial, breadth-height 95.07 or metriocranial, fronto-parietal 67.61 or metriometopic, upper facial 52.14 or mesene, nasal 50.00 or mesorrhine, left orbital 72.73 and 78.05 chamaeconch or mesoconch, depending on which measurement is used. All proportions are, therefore, of the intermediate classes: the brain case width in relation to the length is intermediate, the head is medium high in relation to both the breadth and the length, the forehead is medium in relation to the breadth of the skull, the face is of medium proportions, as is the nose, and the orbits are low to medium.

"*Comparisons:* Morphologically, the skull can be grouped with the northeastern long-heads which have a distribution from Illinois to New England, and generally represent an older substratum of the population in the eastern United States. In the southeastern states this race underlies a more round-headed population that in most cases spoke Muskhogean. It must not be forgotten, however, that this more long-headed element survived in some regions till the advent of the Whites."

not covered with red paint, as they are in some burials. The teeth in some skeletons were in good condition and in others badly worn. Mr. Burch insisted that at least one of the adult skeletons was equipped with two rows of teeth! Reports of large skeletons and unusual tooth arrangement seem to be common in connection with finds of this character. In children of eleven years of age or younger, the new teeth and those in occlusion might make it appear that the individual had two distinct rows of teeth. Occasionally, the teeth of adults are so irregularly spaced as to make it appear that there are two rows of teeth. In the skull in which the lower jaw is missing, the arrangement of the teeth is normal.

In addition to the five skeletons mentioned, other skeletons were unearthed from time to time, for the hauling of gravel from the deposit continued. It is estimated that there were ten skeletons, but very little attention was paid to the finding of human bones after the discovery of the first five skeletons mentioned.

LIST OF ARTICLES

Copper

Among the artifacts was a copper awl, five inches long and three-sixteenths of an inch thick at the widest part (square section), tapering to a point at each end (Pl. I, Fig. 4). An oblong copper gorget, four and three-quarters inches long, one and five-eighths inches wide, and about one-sixteenth of an inch in thickness, with a perforation about one and one-half inches from each end, was also found (Pl. I, Fig. 3). An examination indicates that the perforations were punched instead of drilled. The late George A. West[7] and other members of the staff of the Milwaukee Public Museum stated that this gorget was made of beaten Lake Superior copper. Seventeen copper beads, averaging one-eighth to one-quarter of an inch long and three-sixteenths of an inch in diameter, appear to have been hammered (Pl. I, Fig. 2).

[7] Personal communication, George A. West, late of Milwaukee, Wisconsin.

Shell Beads

In addition to the copper articles there were many shell disk beads, of which 113 were saved. These beads are approximately one-quarter to three-eighths of an inch in diameter and average about one-eighth of an inch in thickness (Pl. I, Fig. 1).

Shell Gorgets

Of three concavo-convex circular or disk shell gorgets, the smallest is three inches in diameter and the largest, three and one-quarter inches. Each gorget has three perforations, the center one being approximately three-sixteenth of an inch in diameter, and the two near the edge of each disk, about one-eighth of an inch in diameter and approximately five-eighths of an inch apart (Pl. I, Figs. 5–7). One of these disks is of a greenish hue, stained from having been in contact with one of the copper pieces, and the other is still colored with red paint. The perforations near the edge of each show evidence of wear; these gorgets probably were suspended on a thong.

Such shell disks are not uncommon in other parts of the United States, though they are seldom found as far north as Michigan, with the exception of a few from Canada.

Three shell gorgets, two with ends broken off and the third with only a small part remaining, were also recovered (Pl. II, Figs. 1–3). They may have been broken when they were being excavated, since most of the broken surfaces do not appear ancient. The largest one in its present condition, with a part missing from one end, is five and one-half inches long and has three perforations. With the natural curvature of the shell from which it was manufactured, it has the appearance of a modern arch support. The next in size, which plainly shows the remains of red paint, has two perforations, and part of one end is missing. The third piece, most of which is missing, is slightly less than four inches long. There is a perforation about one and one-half inches from the unbroken end, and evidence of two perforations side-by-side at the broken end, neither of these being in line with the perforations near the unbroken end. There is the possibility that one or both of the side-by-side perforations may have been drilled for the purpose of binding two or more broken pieces together, as illustrated by the sandal-sole shell gorget from Canada (Pl. V), which has several small perforations for binding the two broken pieces together.

The three broken shell gorgets, all curved conforming to the shells from which they were cut, appear to be a form halfway between the sandal-sole type and the oblong gorget with two perforations (later described). One of the broken gorgets still has red paint on its surface.

Outstanding among the artifacts are two oblong shell gorgets; one is six inches long and one and three-fourths inches wide at the widest part, and the other is six and one-half inches long and two inches wide at the widest part. Both taper toward the ends. Both are flat on one surface and curved on the other, and both have two perforations, one being one-third of the length of the gorget from one end and the other the same distance from the other end. The holes are drilled from the flat surface, although the curved surface bears evidence that they were slightly countersunk from that side. These two gorgets are heavy and solid, about three-sixteenths of an inch thick, and in an excellent state of preservation (Pl. II, Figs. 4–5).

Sandal-Sole or Moccasin-Last Shell Gorgets

In addition to the articles mentioned, five shell gorgets, each with three perforations (with the exception of the largest one), and each shaped like a sandal sole, were found near the heads of the skeletons (Pl. III, Figs. 1–5). This type of shell artifact is sometimes referred to as a "moccasin last." The smallest of these unusual shell articles is slightly less than seven inches long and two and three-fourths inches wide at the widest part near the "toe" end. Each of these sandal soles conforms to the natural curve of the shell from which it was carved. The largest of this type is nine and one-half inches long and three and one-half inches wide. The three perforations are along the middle line, two near the "toe" end not over an inch apart and the third about half way from each end. At least two of these gorgets show slight evidence at the "toe" perforations of having been worn or used.

The largest one differs from the other four in that it has a fourth perforation near the "heel" end within one-sixteenth of an inch of the edge. This perforation has been carefully drilled from the bottom side and is no larger than the point of a lead pencil on the upper or concave side.

This type of gorget is rare. So far as is known, very few sandal-sole shell gorgets have been found in Michigan. Donald Boudeman, of Kalamazoo, Michigan, acquired two when he purchased the Van Wormer collection many years ago. Both are labeled as having been taken from a mound in Branch County, Michigan. Both are broken, but enough remains of each to show clearly that they are of the same type as those from the Coldwater site. Apparently, these two artifacts are from the same gravel deposit described in this article.

Shell Gorgets with Six Perforations

Perhaps the most unusual artifacts from this site, but not with the skeletons, are two shell gorgets, exactly alike and with six perforations each. Both are a segment of an irregular hollow frustum of a concavo-convex cone (Pl. III, Figs. 4–5). Each gorget is two and one-half inches long, one inch wide in the narrowest part, and one and seven-eighths inches wide at the widest diameter. The larger curved end has five small perforations evenly spaced along its edge. A larger perforation appears near the center. All perforations were drilled from the concave side. None of them shows any evidence of wear. The curved margin with the five perforations is slightly over one-sixteenth of an inch thick, and the smaller end is about one-fourth of an inch thick.

Before the discovery of the skeletons mentioned, a public road had been laid over a part of the mound or knoll. Either during the grading of this road or when gravel was being taken from the knoll, a copper axe or celt was found, and at another time a sandal-sole gorget was discovered. This was associated with human bones. Neither of these artifacts can be described, for they have not, to date, been located. The axe may not have been with human bones. The two shell gorgets with six perforations each were not with skeletal remains. No pottery or sherds of any kind were in the gravel deposit or near by.

The two identical shell pieces are considered extremely rare. They were found some distance from the skeletons. So far as can be learned from the larger museums of the Middle West and from the United States National Museum and the American Museum of Natural History, similar articles are not in their collections.

Three different theories have been advanced as to the use of the unusual twin shell pieces. The pieces might have been lashed or tied together at the perforated margins to form a boat stone or gorget; they might have been worn on the head as feather spreaders, the curve of the shell fitting over the braid of hair and a feather being fastened at each of the five perforations in fanlike arrangement; or they might have been used as ear ornaments.

In the event that W. S. Webb and W. G. Haag[8] are correct in concluding that boat stones and other artifacts were used as atlatl weights, and if that were the sole use of boat stones, then the theory of the two shell artifacts forming a boat stone would probably have to be abandoned.

The feather spreader theory may be borne out by the following quotation from a letter written by William Penn to his friends in England:

> They wore ear-rings and nose-jewels; bracelets on their arms and legs, rings on their fingers, necklaces made of highly polished shells found in their rivers and on their coasts. The females tied up their hair behind, worked bands round their heads, and *ornamented them with shells and feathers*, and wore strings of beads round several parts of their bodies. Round their moccasins they had shells and turkey spurs, to tinkle like little bells as they walked.[9]

[8] Webb and Haag, 1939.

[9] W. J. Wintemberg, 1908, pp. 63–64.

RELATED SITES

THE HARRISON SITE

One June 22, 1910, the late Orlin Harrison found in a gravel pit on his farm in Wakeshma Township, Kalamazoo County, Michigan, a flexed burial, with which was a broken sandal-sole shell gorget with the usual three perforations, one irregular shell gorget about three and one-half inches long and averaging one and one-half inches wide with one perforation, one broken shell gorget about five inches long and averaging one and one-half inches wide with five perforations, and one banded slate bird stone (Pl. IV, Fig. 1). The shell gorget with five perforations may have been a sandal sole, for one end is curved similar to the "heel" end of the regular sandal sole and the "toe" end is broken. Three of the five perforations conform very closely to the regular pattern used in the sandal soles.

This find is unusual in that the slate bird stone is said to have been placed crossways on the skull. A somewhat similar birdstone (Pl. IV, Fig. 2) from east-central Indiana was in a context highly suggestive of the Glacial Kame culture.

This information was obtained by Donald Boudeman, of Kalamazoo, Michigan, from the widow of Mr. Harrison and from his son, O. M. Harrison. The artifacts are now in the collection of Clark Steinbarger of Mendon, Michigan.

As is usual in the case of accidental finds, and especially those made many years ago, it is difficult to learn much of scientific value from this material.

THE ZIMMERMAN SITE[10]

On the farm of Arthur Zimmerman, in McDonald Township, about three miles north of Belle Center near the Logan County line but in Hardin County, Ohio, is a huge gravel kame. It is the highest point in the neighborhood, and from the top of it one can see for a distance of twelve to fifteen miles. I visited the site and obtained the following information from Mr. Zimmerman.

[10] Greenman, 1931.

In the summer of 1931 when gravel was being hauled from this pit, 148 human skeletons were discovered from six feet to twenty-two feet below the surface; badly decayed human bones were uncovered about three and one-half feet from the surface, but no complete skeletons were buried at depths less than six feet. Mr. Zimmerman stated that in addition to the 148 skeletons counted, an unknown number was removed in his absence.

The area in which the skeletons were discovered was approximately one hundred by two hundred feet. Most of the kame is still undisturbed. Some of the skeletons were buried face down. John S. B. Matson reported this type of burial from another site in Hardin County.[11] Others appear to have been buried "standing up," and still others were in a sitting position. The outlines of the individual graves were easily determined owing to the fact that they were of darker soil than was the surrounding gravel. Most of the graves, especially the deeper ones, were narrower at the bottom than at the top. With the skeleton in the deepest grave were 148 shell disk beads. Three skeletons of adults were in one grave. In every grave in which the skeletons were in good condition, a light brown substance was associated with the skeletal remains. In the deeper burials, in which copper was present, the skeletal remains were not well preserved.

According to the story, two skeletons of giant size, one male and one female, were found. Notwithstanding the reportedly large skeleton, the skull of the female was no larger than that of a child. Many of the associated artifacts were sold and scattered. Dr. C. J. Bondley, of Belle Center, Ohio, may have the largest part of them in his collection. A little charcoal was observed, and fourteen or more sandal-sole gorgets were discovered "on the front of the skeletons about the middle."

A bell-shaped stone pestle, a wooden bow at a depth of eight or ten feet too badly decayed to preserve, and, near the bow, flint arrowheads were uncovered. Two small pots were found, but one was broken during the excavating.

The Zimmerman site was visited by Emerson F. Greenman,

[11] Whittlesey and Read, 1877, p. 127.

and he described it briefly in a popular account in *Museum Echoes*.[12] He pointed out some of the cultural characteristics and suggested a general relationship to the Hopewell culture.

The Bondley collection of artifacts (Pl. VIII) from the Zimmerman site includes thirteen sandal-sole shell gorgets, or parts thereof, one of which is engraved; six rectangular shell two-hole gorgets, one with the design of a snake upon it; 144 copper beads from three-sixteenths to seven-eighths of an inch in diameter; a tapered slate tube six and one-half inches long; one flint arrowhead; one small slate bead; one small, perforated elk tooth; two perforated fresh-water clam shells; one small grit-tempered Woodland pot, which, according to James B. Griffin, is too small and too generalized to admit of any specific identification; one large marine gastropod identified by Griffin as a *Cassis* specimen and said to have been found on the head of a skeleton; one shell cut in imitation of an animal jaw; and other small articles. Some of the shell artifacts had been broken and later repaired by drilling new holes and binding the pieces together. It is said that most of the sandal-sole shell gorgets were around the shoulders and necks of the skeletons.

THE RIDGEWAY SITE

John S. Matson[13] reported an important find of shell artifacts made in 1856 in Hardin County, Ohio. This report is referred to by Holmes.[14] Because the articles are so similar to those discovered in Michigan (Pl. IX), the following information from that report is set forth at length:

> DEAR SIR: In the fall of 1856, in Hardin county, Ohio, near the Bellefontaine and Indiana Railway, between Mt. Victory and Ridgeway, I commenced removing a gravel bank for the purpose of ballasting a part of the above named railroad. I learned shortly after my arrival there, that the bank was an ancient burial-ground. This information caused me to examine the ground, and note discoveries.
>
> Before I came on the ground, there had been a track graded and

[12] Greenman, 1931, p. 55.

[13] Whittlesey and Read, 1877, pp. 126–30.

[14] Holmes, 1883, p. 265.

laid. This track separated a short distance east of the mound, one track on the south, and the other on the north. The men who graded the track, had taken the loam off where the track ran, and cast it out from the mound. We removed the gravel from both sides, moving the track up to the bank, when it became difficult to load. The loading was done by men with shovels into gravel cars, and hauled out with an engine. The average amount removed was about two hundred and twenty cubic yards per day. About six weeks in the winter we had to suspend operations, on account of freezing. The mound covered an area of *one and a half acres;* being covered with an orchard of apple trees, then in bearing. Several stumps and a few trees of the original forest still remained on the mound. I was informed by citizens of the vicinity that there had been a remarkably heavy growth of timber on the mound. The stumps remaining were large. The mound was what I would call double; the larger and higher part to the west. About two-thirds of the mound was embraced in this part. The eastern part presenting the appearance of a smaller hill having been pressed against the other, leaving a depression between them of three or four feet below the highest point of the smaller and five or six feet below a corresponding point of the larger. Both parts had the appearance of having had surface work done, to give them a beautiful oval shape. The loam I found deepest on the highest points, where it is generally of less depth. The interior was composed of a clean limestone gravel and sand, evidently formed by decomposition of the strata, and very plainly marked. In the eastern or smaller part of the mound was an excavation that had been made by citizens of the vicinity for sand for building purposes, in which excavation I learned a number of skeletons had been exhumed having beads and trinkets on, which were reported as being similar to those I afterward found. I was unable to obtain any of them. A little south of the highest point of the western mound was an excavation made by the railroad company for the purpose of ascertaining the amount of gravel. No remains were found in that excavation. Shortly after commencing to load gravel, indications of graves were visible in three places, on both sides of the eastern part, and nearly north of the center of the larger or western part. At the last named place, two skeletons, side by side, were found in a horizontal position; the feet pointing east, which had been deposited there without their heads, there being no evidence of skulls. With them I found a stone axe or celt of granite, two flint arrow points, and an implement made of blue stone resembling slate, but much harder, the outlines of which I give full size; also a large fresh water clam, filled with red paint, in good preservation.* The flint implements had the appearance of never having been used, being very sharp-pointed. The bones crumbled on exposure to the atmosphere. These graves were about four feet deep. The first skeletons taken out of the eastern part of the mound were in better preservation, especially those on the south side. Several skulls were sound, and the other bones of some were so well preserved that, by applying sole leather for ribs, they were wired together. With the first skeleton taken out of this part of the mound, I found a thin piece of ivory, with two small holes, evidently an ear ornament. Next was the skeleton of a little girl, who may have been eight or ten years old. Skull in good preservation, which remains in my cabinet. She had a string of beads, so made as to be larger in the center of the neck in front, tapering almost to a point at the back of the neck; she also had a plate of copper on her neck. The lower maxillary and upper joints of the vertebra are yet green from its oxidation. The plate had two rows of dents a part of the way around. The dents look like an impression made on a board with the heel of a boot with tacks. The two last skeletons had been buried in a sitting posture. In the north side, nearly opposite the last named skeletons, was a grave about four feet deep, in which the remains had been deposited and apparently burned. There were ashes and charcoal, with pieces of charred bones, one or two of the hands being entire.

In the progress of removal, I found the eastern or small part of the mound to be literally filled with graves. The modes of burial had been various; the depth of remains varying from two to nine feet; while there was a difference of posture in nearly every skeleton. I found that not less than ten or twelve dogs had also been buried; the human and canine side by side. One group of nine graves I was so impressed with, I will endeavor to be particularly explicit. The first had two skeletons, that of a male and female, side by side, there not being more than four inches of sand between them. Both had evidently been buried in one grave. The female was buried on her knees, both hands spread over the face, which was downwards, and a string of conch shell beads around her neck. I found inside of her ribs the remains of a foetus. Her partner was buried horizontal, with face down; both hands had been placed with their palms on the face, their heads toward the east. After tracing the bones with particular reference to their positions, and to

* The celt is eight inches long, and the blue slate stone two and three-fourths. It is of a common form flat, with two tapering holes near the middle.

save these skeletons which were best preserved, I took down the disturbed strata with my hands; and at the head of the grave I found above the remains, and pointing down, the bones of the index finger, while at the foot of the grave, and at a corresponding height, the bones of a great toe, pointing in a similar manner. The balance of the group were buried some with face down, both hands over the face, others with one hand; some with face up, and both hands over the face; while another had one hand over the breast, the other over the face. All this group had the heads to the east. On one of this group, I found a string of copper beads, of which the metal had never been smelted, but evidently had been flaked from the native metal, and rolled around a twisted string, evidence of which was still visible in the beads, which were rude. On the north side of the eastern portion, under an oak tree stump (one hundred and fifty years old by growths), were the remains of the largest human bones I had ever seen. The joints of the vertebra seemed as large as those of a horse. I think they did not indicate a taller frame than some others; but the bones were heavier than any in the mound. I have its inferior maxillary broken, but glued together, in my cabinet. The other bones were so decomposed that they were useless. I could not say as to his posture, as the stump brought down the grave, rendering it out of the question to note the position. Near the last named skeleton, perhaps ten feet from it, we came upon a grave that had been dug oblong almost six feet deep, three feet wide, and over seven feet long, which they had filled with human bones promiscuously, without regard to order, to the depth of four feet; on these, in regular order, were placed twenty-seven skulls, with the top of skulls up. They were about two feet below the surface; the bones so much broken, and I regret to say I did not examine them as particular as I should have done. One of the skulls had a small hole broken in, and I learned afterward that a piece of the femur was found where they were dumped on the road having a flint dart fast in the bone. There was an implement or ornament found having one part like the head of a bird's neck, and shoulders like a horse, cut off back of the shoulders, and turned up like the back part of a saddle seat; the lower part being flat, with a hole drilled diagonally from the lower part of the neck to the base, with a corresponding hole in the back part. This implement was manufactured of a blue stone resembling slate, but extremely hard.*

* This is the saddle-shaped stone figured on page 239 of Squier and Davis' *Monuments of the Mississippi Valley*. It is either an ornament or a badge, which was suspended, and is frequently found on the surface. [These are now called birdstones.]

It is probable they had had a battle, and after the flesh had decomposed, they collected the bones and brought them to the mound for burial. I am sure from the positions of the bones, they had not been interred with the flesh on. I found in this part of the mound the remains of at least fifty children, under the age of eight years, some with two, others with four incisors, some with eight, and others with no teeth. On the neck of one infant having two incisors, there was a string of conch shell beads of the largest size, one hundred and forty in number; four of these beads were black, and were about three-fourths of an inch in diameter. The string would weigh one pound or more. Some of the graves had trinkets and beads made of clam shell; some had bones of the deer, sharp-pointed, others had pieces of deer horns; some had long-shaped beads around the wrists, I think of ivory. One had a conch shell plate (Plate XII, Fig. C)[16a] round, about five inches in diameter, with a hole in the center, half an inch in diameter, with two holes near the edge, for suspension with a string from the neck, like a breast-plate. Some had birds buried with them. One skeleton taken out of this part of the mound had the appearance of a very aged man; the point of the inferior maxillary was almost in two parts, while the trachea was bone all around. Quite a number showed indications of extreme age; seven or eight that I observed had bone tracheas.

I now return to the western or larger portion of the mound. This part was removed as fast as the former. I soon discovered there were two rows of graves, leading direct from the *two first mentioned*, containing the flint implements, paint, etc., towards the center, each pair having been dug deeper as they approached the center of the mound. Those with the stone axe, paint, and flint implements were four feet deep, the depth of each pair increasing about a foot in regular gradation till the last pair, which was as near the center and highest point of the mound as I could calculate, the last pair being *eighteen feet* below the surface. The pair next to those with the axe, paint and flint implements were in a sitting posture, as were all in these two files except the first two. On the head of one of the second pair was a conch shell plate (Plate XII, Fig. A)[16a] resembling in shape the sole of a moccasin, nine inches in length and three and a half inches greatest breadth. This plate has three holes in it towards the wider end, and it was placed on the top of the head, with the larger end back. Two other skeletons of these two files had similar plates (Plate XII, Fig. B),[16a] differing only in size, the smaller being about half the size of the

[16a] See Plate IX.

larger. Several implements of stone were found, all differing in shape. They were of stone resembling slate, but much harder. One of them is three inches long by one and a half broad, in form of a shield, with two holes through it flatwise. Farmers picked up some implements in the field adjoining the mound. One given me by Judge Baldwin is a flat stone of slate, with one transverse hole, that I supposed belonged to the same race. As we approached the center of the mound, the graves getting deeper, the bones were much better preserved. Several bodies in decomposition had formed a cement that would have preserved them an almost incalculable length of time. In fact, when first taken out of the cement they had the appearance of bones just dissected, being nearly one-third heavier than those without cement. The four last deepest skeletons *all* had beads on, some of them quite small, the smallest not as large as a pea. Some were made of clam shells, but mostly of conch or sea shells. Those of clam were so decomposed that they fell to pieces. Three of these skeletons had beads, only around the neck, the fourth, being the last one taken out, and the file leader (as he ought to be called), of the two deepest, had, I should think, nearly thirty yards of beads, having four wraps around the neck crossed over the breast and back, passing down between his legs; strings down his legs to the feet; also strings along his arms and around his wrists. This remains presented the appearance of being decorated all over. He had no other ornaments or implements that I could find. Near the south side of the western part of the mound, near one of the forest trees, I found the remains of a human being that seemed to be detached from all the rest. I thought perhaps he was an Indian of some of the late tribes, who had been buried perhaps on some hunting expedition. There was a piece of deer horn with him that had the appearance of having been the handle of a butcher knife. I could not detect any evidence of rust, however.

On the highest part of the mound, and about twelve or fifteen feet from the two deepest graves, was evidence of fire. The loam had been burned till it had a brick color. I have seen it look very much so where a large log heap had been burned, and would have thought such was the cause, had it not been that it was below the surface about three feet. The whole number of skeletons exhumed by me was *three hundred and eight*. I could not ascertain how many had been taken out by diggers of sand. The citizens of the vicinity informed me that there was a very heavy forest on the mound at the time of clearing it. They also stated that the Indians who were there with the first settlers knew nothing of the race who interred their dead there. I have very little doubt they belonged to the age of stone. There was no evidence that they ever had any communication with the age of iron or bronze. They must have had some commercial arrangements for getting conch shells and copper. The copper has the appearance of the Lake Superior copper, and the conch shells must have come from the Atlantic, Pacific, or Gulf of Mexico. There was no evidence of pottery that I was able to discover. I have visited as many as twenty in the Mississippi Valley, on nearly every one of which were pieces of broken pottery, literally covering the mounds. East of Vicksburg, near Black River, we turned a mound into a redoubt. In excavating, there were layers of charcoal of about two inches in depth in the mound. I found a small stone ax or celt, also a stone shaped like the knob of a bureau. There was a circle hollowed out in the center of the raised part; within the circle was a depression as if the stone had been turned in a lathe on a pivot. This mound was small in area, and not over six feet high. In a south-west direction, and not further than twelve rods, was a smaller mound four feet in height, and south-east from this was a large belt of gravel in the shape of a horse shoe, that had been strewn with shells in sufficient quantities to whiten the ground. About a mile from this, in a north-east direction, across Clear Creek, I visited a mound on which the plough had turned up human bones. But I will not weary you further with Mississippi mounds.[15]

It is noted that the Ridgeway site and the Burch site in Michigan have many traits in common, namely, skeletons in a flexed position, copper beads, copper plates or gorgets, shell beads, red paint, disks perforated in the same manner, sandal-sole shell perforations, position of the shells near the heads of the skeleton, and no evidence of pottery. It should be noted, however, that although stone axes, slate pieces, and flint arrows were found in Hardin County, none have yet been located in the Michigan gravel deposit. This may be accounted for by the fact that the Michigan component has never been thoroughly excavated by an experienced archaeologist.

[15] Holmes, 1883, pp. 126–30.

OTHER SITES IN HARDIN COUNTY, OHIO

Dr. Jesse Snodgrass[16] reported and fully described a carved shell taken in 1886 from the farm of William Spitzer, three and one-half miles northeast of Kenton, Hardin County, Ohio, in a gravel deposit eight or ten rods long and three rods wide. Several human skeletons, slate ornaments, banner stones, arrowheads, were also collected. A piece had been broken from one end of the shell, but from the illustration it appears to be shaped like a sandal sole with the carving of a bear upon its surface. This specimen is now in the collection of the Ohio State Museum (Pl. VI, Fig. 2).[17] Also in this collection from Hardin County is a broken sandal-sole gorget from a gravel bank with a burial (Pl. VI, Fig. 1) from the Otis Stiner farm.

SPECIMENS FROM MERCER COUNTY, OHIO

Perhaps the most comprehensive article on shell artifacts was written by William H. Holmes. The somewhat rare sandal-sole type, similar in all respects to shells from Michigan, is described:

> A remarkable specimen of this class is given in Figure 5. It is made from the body of a large busycon perversum, and is nine and one-half inches long by three inches in width at the widest part. The concave surface has been highly polished, but is now somewhat roughened by weathering; the back has been slightly ground to take off the rougher ridges of growth; the edges are even and rounded and in many places quite thin; the pecularity of its shape is such as to give it very much the appearance of the sole of a sandal. The perforations are three in number, one being near the middle and the others near the broader end, about one and one-half inches apart; they are very neatly made and are slightly bi-conical and a little countersunk. There appears to be no evidence whatever of abrasion by use. It was found associated with human remains in a mound at Sharpsburg, Mercer County, Ohio. A similar specimen from the same locality is nearly nine inches in length. As in the specimen illustrated, one perforation is placed near the middle and two others near the

[16] Snodgrass, 1894, pp. 114–15.

[17] See also Moorehead, 1900, Fig. 502.

broader end. This specimen is highly polished on the broader part of the back, and is evenly smoothed on the concave side. It bears evidence of considerable use, and the two holes are much worn by a string or cord, which, passing from one hole to another on the concave side of the plate, gradually worked a deep groove between them. On the back of the convex side, the perforations show no evidence of wear. The central perforation is not worn on either side. The letter of Mr. Whitney transmitting this relic to the National Museum, states that there were in the mound "about ten pairs of the shell sandals of different sizes, and made to fit the right and left feet." From the latter remark, I should infer that some were made from dextral and others from sinistral shells; the two described are made from the busycon perversum.[18]

At least a part of this letter of transmittal has been published:

Whitney, J. L., writing from Rose Hill, Ohio, speaks of copper axes and shell objects from a mound half a mile from Sharpsburg, Mercer County, Ohio. Ten pairs of shell relics were found resembling the bottoms of sandals. The mounds at this point are composed of sand and gravel. A large quantity of shell beads, a copper axe, and the skeleton of a tall man were recovered from the same mound. There are several mounds at this point composed of sand and gravel. The largest contains a quantity of very fine grayish-white sand, very hard, and streaked with bands of pure, white sand.[19]

From the description it is difficult to tell whether these finds were from an artificial mound or from a natural knoll. In view of the testimony of the other finds the probability is that they were not taken from a true mound. The large number of specimens is somewhat unusual. Probably some of those now in various collections labeled only Mercer County, Ohio, came from this deposit. The Museum of the American Indian, Heye Foundation, New York City, has in its collections a sandal-sole shell gorget (Cat. No. 8/8356) of the regular type, from Sharpsburg, Mercer County, Ohio.[20]

[18] Holmes, 1883, pp. 264–65.

[19] Mason, 1881, p. 448. This site must be very close to the Fox-Rammel gravel pits discussed below.

[20] E. K. Burnett, personal communication.

A sandal-sole gorget reported by Moorehead in 1895 came into the possession of James Pillars in 1892. It is labeled as having been "found by John Smith, in gravel bank or mound, Mercer County, Ohio."[21] Another gorget from Mercer County was also illustrated by Moorehead with the following caption: "Fig. 503 is from the collection of James Pillars, Lima, Ohio. It was found in a mound, Mercer County, Ohio. There are three perforations."[22] The perforations in this gorget are slightly different from those from the Burch site in that the two perforations near the toe end are farther apart, and the one near the heel end is nearer the edge.

The Fort Recovery Banking Co., of Fort Recovery, Ohio, has in its collection ten sandal-sole shell gorgets, nine with the usual three perforations and one with four perforations, one shell disk gorget with the usual three perforations, one shell disk with thirteen perforations, two oblong shell gorgets, one with two perforations and the other with five, and some shell disk beads and copper beads. All were associated with skeletal remains. One skeleton was said to have had a thick covering "which resembled felt." At least one skeleton was in a flexed position. Some skeletons were found at a depth of three to four feet; one, an extended burial, is said to have been at least fifteen feet deep. Charcoal was present in many places with the skeletons. There was no evidence of red paint. Some of the artifacts in this collection were in the Alex Fox gravel pit, and the rest were in the Leonard Rammel gravel pit, both pits being in the southeastern part of Gibson Township, Mercer County, Ohio. This find was made accidently about 1935 in a glacial gravel deposit, and the information obtained is hearsay.

Two shell gorgets of the sandal-sole type labeled "Ft. Recovery, Mercer County, Ohio" were formerly in the Payne collection. One is nine and one-half inches long and two and seven-eighths inches wide (Pl. VI, Fig. 3); the other is nine and one-eighth inches long and two and seven-eighths inches wide

[21] Moorehead, 1895, pp. 146–47.

[22] Moorehead, 1900, p. 344.

(Pl. VI, Fig. 5).[23] Another specimen in Meyer's collection obtained from the Payne estate is labeled as "from a grave in Putnam County, Ohio." It is eight and one-half inches long and two and one-quarter inches wide and is thus much narrower than any other I have seen. There is some indication of slight wear at both perforations near the toe end (Pl. VI, Fig. 6).

Two other sandal-sole gorgets are in the W. M. Cunningham collection. They are labeled "Fort Recovery, Mercer County, Ohio" and "Darke County, Ohio." No information of any kind as to the circumstances under which they were found could be obtained when they were purchased.

In the American Museum of Natural History there are two circular shell gorgets with a central hole and two marginal holes for suspension at the top of the gorget. These specimens and a string of fifty flat disk-shape shell beads were with a burial in a "mound" on the farm of Dan Snyder near St. Johns in Auglaize County, Ohio. This burial was one of eight uncovered at the site. The specimens are part of the Douglas collection.

Another engraved gorget from northern Ohio is illustrated by Moorehead, who described it:

> "Fig. 526 (S. 1–2) An engraved shell gorget found in the glacial kame burials in northern Ohio. This is shown half-size and is a remarkable specimen. The material is from a large freshwater Unio.[24]

If Moorehead's identification of the shell as "fresh-water Unio" is correct it will be even more remarkable, for almost all of these specimens are made from marine gastropods. From the photograph it is apparent that the gorget is about six inches long and three inches wide. The arrows are engraved on the shell and are formed by three closely spaced narrow lines.

A part of an engraved shell gorget, five and one-half inches long and three and one-half inches wide, was recently presented to me by Harvey E. Bouwknegt, of Grandville, Michigan. The

[23] I am indebted to Mr. Richard K. Meyer of Peoria, Illinois, for permission to reproduce these specimens.

[24] Moorehead, 1910, II: 124.

only information available is a notation that it was from a gravel bank in Mercer County, Ohio. On the basis of comparison with similar gorgets it must have been originally nine and one-half inches long. Most of the "heel" end is missing. This piece has the usual three perforations, and the two near the "toe" end are somewhat worn. The end at which the break occurred has been carefully smoothed. The design covers the inside, or concave, surface of the shell. It was apparently made by a very sharp instrument as fine as a needle of today. It consists of a series of lines of minute depressions, in some places three and in others four in width, making a row. Each row is about one-eighth of an inch wide, and the rows are separated by a space of about one-eighth of an inch. The design begins near the center of the shell and moves in a series of circular rows toward the outer edges. There are two such circular designs, and an examination indicates that there was a third one on the missing part. As mentioned above, the Bondley collection includes an engraved sandal-sole shell gorget and an engraved rectangular shell gorget.

GLACIAL KAME SITES IN INDIANA

The Ohio State Museum has in its collections three sandal-sole gorgets from Randolph County, Indiana (Pl. VII, Figs. 1–3). At the time these objects were acquired the following information was obtained:

> On the farm of Thomas J. Mulen, 5 miles north of Winchester, in Ward Township, south side of Mud Creek, a tributary of the Mississinewa River, in 1885, an extensive prehistoric burying ground was brought to light. The site is an extensive gravel deposit, and the discovery of the burying ground came through the opening of a gravel bank in constructing a roadway.
>
> A solid acre of gravel was removed, in places to a depth of 16 to 18 feet. More than 100 skeletons were unearthed, interment as a rule being beyond the usual depth, workmen stating that they had noticed skeletal remains as deep as 12 feet below the surface.
>
> Some remarkable objects, mostly of shell, were found, and were for the most part retained by Mr. T. J. Mulen, owner of the farm,

who in 1902 donated them to Mr. C. M. Young. The objects herewith were found with five separate skeletons, being placed mostly about the head and shoulders. The material comprises three shell disks, with a large perforation in the center, and two smaller ones near the edge, which showed decided strong wear; three spoon-shaped or sole-shaped shell pieces, with a hole near the center, and two small holes near the edge at the rounded ends. One of these pieces is marked near the smaller end with incised lines, resembling a series of the letter X, thus XXXXXXXX; another has a most interesting and intricate figure or design incised on the concave face, suggesting an elaborate cross design. A triangular section had been broken from the specimen, which included the upper corner of the figure, and this while missing when the find was made, had previously been repaired, as shown by some neat counter-sinking of holes for receiving a cord. A gorget of the rectangular type common in slate, but made of shell is another of the objects; this has two perforations. A huge bowl or container, capacity about 1 gallon, also of shell, a tube of the tobacco pipe type, and a finely polished celt of black slate; a string of very large shell beads and a large string of smaller shell beads, button-shaped, complete the remarkable find.[25]

It should be observed that one of these gorgets (Pl. VII, Fig. 1) has an elaborate cross (?) design, which was engraved on the forward end of the specimen, with an apparent functional connection with the three perforations. This engraving is a closely spaced three-line style which is identical with that on the gorget from northern Ohio and similar to that employed on pottery vessels of Natchezan style in the lower Mississippi Valley.

A vague and unsatisfactory reference to a possible find in Indiana was given by Moorehead, when he wrote: "Mr. John N. Hodgin, of Richmond, Indiana, writes that he found some fifteen or twenty shell ornaments like this one in a grave."[26]

In the Museum of the American Indian, Heye Foundation, there are two sandal-sole shell gorgets. They were associated with a platform pipe (Pl. X, Fig. 1) and a circular shell gorget with one perforation in a grave ten feet deep in a gravel pit in

[25] Richard G. Morgan, personal communication.

[26] Moorehead, 1900, p. 344.

Allen County, Indiana.[27] Except for the fact that the edges of the sandal-sole artifacts are rough and broken in places, they resemble the regular type. Both have the usual three perforations, and one of them has a fourth perforation near the edge, very similar to that in one of the sandal-sole gorgets from the Burch site, except that the perforation in the Allen County specimen is not as small as in the one from Michigan.

One of the most recent archaeological finds to be linked with the Glacial Kame complex has been made at Cedar Point on the shores of Lake Wawasee, Kosciusko County, Indiana:

> The body was in a flexed position, a "sandal sole" shaped shell gorget 9⅛ inches long with four perforations was on the chest. It was buried ten feet below the old ground level. There were no artifacts except the gorget. It was observed, however, that there was "just below the smaller end of the gorget, and running underneath it, a very dark brown or black deposit interwoven with a fibrous substance like roots which may have been the last traces of some wooden implement or a tool handle." Copper had been present as there were deep green copper stains on leg and arm bones.[28]

A find made in 1923 at this site consisted of circular shell gorgets with a large central perforation one-half to two-thirds of an inch across and with two closely spaced marginal holes. These gorgets had been placed with eight human skeletons and the bones of a dog; it is estimated they were buried eight feet beneath the surface. A find made in 1882 yielded a British halfpenny dated 1795 and associated with a burial; the coin was enclosed in a globular mass of green earth:

> A somewhat more serious archaeological "dig" on this location was conducted in 1931 through the courtesy of Mr. Snook. Five broken

[27] E. K. Burnett, personal communication. This pipe is illustrated in Moorehead (1910, II: 47). It is also illustrated in West (1934, II: Pl. 52, 1 and 3). West has identified the Indiana pipe as from Scioto County, Ohio, and the Ohio pipe as from Indiana. According to West the Allen County pipe is of red Ohio pipestone.

[28] Lilly, 1942, p. 32.

and burned rock fire places, a deeply buried semi-circle of stones set in clay and a shallow infant burial accompanied by one of the characteristic shell gorgets was about all that was discovered.[29]

SANDAL-SOLE GORGETS FROM ILLINOIS

Another sandal-sole gorget with three perforations, in the collection of B. W. Stephens, of Quincy, Illinois, is said to have been taken from the surface at a village site along the Illinois River in Morgan County.[30] The perforations are unworn.

From the west side of the Illinois River another sandal-sole gorget is reported from a mound on a narrow ridge near the mouth of Sugar Creek, between Frederick and Browning, Schuyler County, Illinois. Approximately twenty years ago this mound was excavated by Charles L. Harris, of Macomb, Illinois, who described the mound as probably artificial and constructed of limey loess. An oblong shell gorget about eight and one-half inches long and four inches wide, with three perforations, had been struck by a plow before it was excavated, and one corner was broken off. A second shell gorget, with three perforations, was about nine and one-half inches long, three and three-quarters inches wide, and shaped like a sandal sole. This shell piece was heavily coated on one side with a lime deposit:

> This shell piece when found was on top of the skull, the large concave end cupping over the frontal bone and the more pointed end extending back over the crown of the skull.[31]

The body had been buried on its back. Five skeletons were in this mound. Two copper awls were found, one of which still had about one inch of handle, probably of deer antler. There was no evidence of flexed burials, red paint, ashes, cremated bones, or pottery. The two shell artifacts were purchased by Mr. Payne, of Springfield, Illinois, about 1917.

Charles Harris reported also that graves near by yielded coiled copper beads, a stone platform pipe, the shell of a box

[29] Lilly, 1942, p. 31.

[30] B. W. Stephens, personal communication.

[31] Charles Harris, of Macomb, Illinois, personal communication.

turtle filled with small white pebbles, fifteen leaf-shaped flints, and a copper awl eleven inches long. On each side of the head of one body in a near by mound there was a skull.

In the collection of R. K. Meyer, purchased from the Payne collection, is a shell gorget labeled, "Dixon Mound, Illinois River, Macomb, Illinois." It is eight and one-half inches long, three and one-quarter inches wide, and gradually curved at each end; although it has three perforations, they are spaced differently than are the perforations in the sandal-sole gorgets (Pl. VI, Fig. 7). This may have been the gorget found by Charles L. Harris. A sandal-sole gorget in the same collection is labeled "Kahokia Mound, Illinois" (Pl. VI, Fig. 4).

RELATED SITES IN ONTARIO

In 1849, John McDowell, while digging for a foundation of a house on the east side of Blackfriar's bridge, which is now part of the city of London, Ontario, discovered a grave which yielded a number of shell gorgets, a shell pendant, a copper bead, one cylindrical shell bead, eight discoidal shell beads, and one heart-shaped shell pendant.[32] One of the shell gorgets was a sandal sole, and it is now in the Royal Ontario Museum of Archaeology at Toronto (No. 9771).[33] Three broken disk shell gorgets and two unbroken ones were also unearthed. One of these was stained a deep rich green from having been in contact with copper.

In 1907, a single grave was discovered by Edward Redmond in a gravel pit at the west end of the village of Weston, York Township, York County, Ontario. The skeleton lay full length in a bed of material resembling red hematite. Around the neck was a string of copper beads, and a copper awl lay near the bones of the right hand.[34] This burial has some traits similar to those of the Michigan find. In several of the burials red paint was reported by Wintemberg.

[32] Wintemberg, 1928, p. 192.

[33] Wintemberg, 1908, p. 54.

[34] *Ibid.*, p. 176.

The Picton Burial

In 1912, George Leslie discovered on the farm of the late James Bedborough, Hallowell Township, Prince Edward County, near Picton, Ontario, a skeleton and the partly cremated bones of a young person, with copper and shell artifacts.[35] There was an extended burial surrounded by a considerable quantity of red paint. Among the articles was a sandal-sole shell gorget (Pl. V), which is now in the National Museum at Ottawa (No. VIIIF17502). It has the usual three perforations in a row across the longer diameter, two near the "toe" end and the third about half way from each end. This gorget had been broken in two pieces, the break extending across the gorget at the edge of the second regular perforation near the "toe" end. It appears that after the break occurred six small perforations were made along each broken edge, each perforation being opposite one on the other part; when the two pieces were placed together they could be lashed or fastened in their original position. Apparently, one perforation was made too near the broken edge, and a small part of shell was broken away, making it necessary to drill another hole farther back from the broken edge.

In the same burial with the sandal-sole gorget were several other articles, such as one circular shell gorget with three perforations, one half round shell gorget, seven discoidal shell beads, one cylindrical shell bead, two copper beads, one copper gouge, one heavy copper axe, four long double-pointed spikes of copper, and a fragment of another spike about a foot long. The bones in this burial were covered with something like decayed bark and a layer of red ochre.[36]

One other sandal-sole shell gorget is in the Stewart collection, now in the Royal Ontario Museum at Toronto (No. 34458), but there is no information respecting its origin.[37] This makes a total of three such gorgets that are known to have been found in Canada, and a fourth that may be presumed to be from there. The three were in artificial graves.

[35] *Ibid.*, pp. 190 ff.

[36] *Ibid.*, p. 177.

[37] *Ibid.*, p. 192, footnote 157.

OTHER RELATED FINDS

There is in the collection of the Museum of the American Indian, Heye Foundation (No. 17/1106), an oval-shaped shell gorget with five perforations; three of them are on the medial line and in the same general position as in the sandal-shaped gorgets, although the shape of the specimen is not that of the northern specimens.[38] This gorget was recovered by Moore[39] from a shell heap by the St. John's River, Florida.

If the Florida example is not quite a classic sandal-sole specimen a recent find from northern Alabama will satisfy all of the specifications, including a muddled record as to its cultural associations. This is accounted for by the authors: "It was quite evident that most of the floor had been dug before. This was easy to explain because of the many local legends concerning 'buried treasure' in the cave."[40]

The objects recovered are listed in the report, and the sandal-sole gorget is illustrated. The pottery is predominantly limestone tempered. Six sherds are Mulberry Creek Plain, two are Wright Check Stamp, and one is Long Branch Fabric Marked. One sherd has crushed rock temper, which is rare in the Tennessee Valley in northern Alabama. It has a plain surface. There are three sherds with a sandy paste. One of these is plain, one is malleated on the exterior but whether this was by a cord-wrapped paddle is not clear, and the third is Alexander Pinched of the style illustrated in the Wheeler basin report.[41] Two shell-tempered sherds, now joined into one, are Mississippi Plain.[42] This statement regarding the pottery varies slightly from that given by Webb and DeJarnette.

The copper gorget, as illustrated in the report, has two rows of repoussé impressions around the outside edge. They were made from the reverse side, whereas the two closely spaced holes

[38] E. K. Burnett, personal communication.

[39] Moore, 1893, p. 718 and Fig. 14.

[40] Webb and DeJarnette, 1942, p. 269.

[41] Webb, 1939, Pl. 122b, No. 6.

[42] The pottery type names are those used in Haag, 1942*a*, except for Mississippi Plain, which designates plain-surfaced shell-tempered pottery.

near the upper central margin were punched from the obverse side. This treatment resembles that reported by Matson from the original Hardin County, Ohio, site. Such repoussé work is rare in Hopewellian copper objects, and the particular artifact type is also rare in Mississippi cultures. The corner and basal notched projectile points illustrated as having been derived from the cave are distinctive, and if actually associated with the shell, copper, and stone gorgets would form a significant culture group. In a neighboring site, where the distinctive projectile points also appear, a circular shell gorget with one central and two marginal perforations was with a flexed burial which was placed in a vertical position.[43]

Even farther afield is the occurrence of stone gorgets with a shape and perforations resembling those in the sandal-sole specimens made of shell. Examples from Texas have not been clearly associated with a definite culture complex.[44]

There is a type of stone gorget found occasionally in Michigan and other states that, because of its shape and style of perforations and its close resemblance to the sandal-sole three-hole shell gorget, may bear some relationship to the shell artifacts.

Stone gorgets of the general sandal shape are not common in Michigan. The one described herein is mentioned because its shape and perforations are similar to those of the sandal-sole shell gorgets (Pl. X, Fig. 2). It was found near Bloomingdale, Van Buren County, Michigan. It is a snowshoe-shaped green-banded slate, seven inches long and two and three-quarters inches wide at the widest part. The three perforations are in the same relative position as those in the shell sandals, and the two near the "toe" end show evidence of wear, as do a few of the shell sandals.

Another three-hole brown slate gorget from Berrien County, Michigan, is five and one-half inches long, two and seven-eighths inches wide, and about one-eighth of an inch thick. It is slightly convex (Pl. X, Fig. 3).

[43] Webb and DeJarnette, 1942, Pl. 152, Fig. 2.

[44] Jackson, 1941, Pl. 3.

A third stone gorget, in the collection of Arthur Bradley,[45] of Lansing, Michigan, is not quite seven inches long and is two and one-quarter inches wide at the widest part, with two perforations near the "toe" end and the third perforation about two inches from the "heel" end. It is much more pointed than are the shell sandals. It was found on the surface about three miles southeast of Ionia, Michigan.

Of the two three-hole, snowshoe-shaped slate gorgets in the collection of Donald Boudeman,[46] of Kalamazoo, one is from Ingham County and the other from Cass County, Michigan. Similar stone gorgets are in other large collections.

Is it a mere coincidence that the stone gorgets were similar in shape to the sandal-sole shell ones and that there were three perforations in the same relative position in each class, or is there a relationship? In western Michigan and northern Indiana stone gorgets of this type are associated with the Hopewellian occupation,[47] and their use seems largely to have died out by the time of the late prehistoric and historic culture groups in the area. The presence of copper and Gulf Coast shell artifacts in Hopewellian is also not to be forgotten in investigating the cultural associations of the Glacial Kame culture.

A cannel coal gorget with three perforations is illustrated and described by James Pillars.[48] It was found in 1889, embedded in a silt deposit about six feet below the surface in Allen County, Ohio. This specimen is eight inches long, two inches wide, and one-half inch thick. It is jet black, polished, much worn, shows considerable use, and has three perforations, two near the small end and one just below the middle. On the face between the two upper holes, which are one-half inch apart, it is much worn to a perceptible depth, evidencing a suspension. There are 438 notches discernible on the corners and edges. This artifact is now in the collection of the Ohio State Museum (No. 57/11). Al-

[45] Arthur Bradley, of Lansing, Michigan, personal communication.

[46] Donald Boudeman, of Kalamazoo, Michigan, personal communication.

[47] For Michigan, see Quimby, 1941, Pl. II, and for Indiana, see McAllister, 1932, Fig. 41.

[48] *The Archaeologist*, III (1895): 146–47.

though this gorget is not of the exact shape of the two Michigan ones mentioned, it has the three perforations in the same general position. Was this type of stone gorget copied after the shell three-hole sandal sole, or vice versa, or were both manufactured during the same period?

Two bone gorgets from the Chilton site in Henry County, Kentucky, are similar in size and shape to the two shell gorgets from Coldwater:

> The information gained from this exploration seems not sufficient to definitely determine the cultural connection of this site. It may be said, however, that the trait complex corresponds most nearly to that found in low stone mounds which are known to be widely distributed in Kentucky, Ohio, West Virginia, Pennsylvania, New York, Tennessee, and Indiana.[49]

There are very few traits in common between the two types of burial. The burials in the Chilton site were in clay, and the bodies were fully extended and covered with limestone slabs; those of the Coldwater site were flexed and buried in a glacial gravel kame.

Probably the outstanding trait of this burial complex is the sandal-sole gorget. The fact that these sandal-shaped specimens were generally found on the head in the few instances for which there is any definite information, leads one to believe that they may have been used to decorate or dress the hair, but were of greater importance and value to the wearer than ordinary hair ornaments, since powers of magic, protection, or authority were undoubtedly attributed to them.

IMPORTANCE OF SHELLS TO HISTORIC INDIANS

There seems to be no doubt but that shells laboriously transported over many miles of wilderness from the Gulf of Mexico or the Atlantic coast were the objects of barter and were highly prized by those who finally acquired them and carved certain objects from them. Schoolcraft commented:

[49] Funkhouser and Webb, 1937, p. 201.

In exchange for the native copper of Lake Superior, and for the brown pipestone of the Chippewa River of the Upper Mississippi, and the blood red pipestone of the Coteau des Prairies west of the St. Peters, they received certain admired species of the sea-shells of the Floridian coasts . . . .[50]

According to Long, the Omaha Indians had in their possession, about three quarters of a century ago, a large shell which had already been transmitted from generation to generation and to which they paid a great deal of veneration. It was considered so sacred that a skin lodge or temple was appropriated for its preservation. In this lodge a person charged with the care of it resided constantly. It was never allowed to touch the earth, and anyone who impiously set eyes on it became blind. This shell was always taken along on their national hunting expeditions and it was also consulted as an oracle.

It is quite natural to suppose that any ornament made of sea-shell would likewise be invested with mystic and protective powers and would be worn primarily as an ornament or charm, and finally, perhaps, losing this significance, the wearing of it for purely decorative purposes became more general; just as much jewelry of the civilized races of today was once supposed to exert a talismanic influence.[51]

The farther these useful articles were carried from the source of supply the greater the value that would attach to them, and far inland the shell of the sea might easily become an object of unusual consideration. Having an origin more or less shrouded in mystery, it would in time become doubly dear to the heart of the superstitious savage, perhaps an object of actual veneration, or at least one of such high esteem that it would be treasured by the living and buried with the dead.

The material so plentiful on the seashore that it was thought of only as it proved useful for vessels and implements, became a valued treasure in the interior; its functions were gradually enlarged and differentiated; it was worked into varied shapes, such as pendants for the ears, beads for the neck, pins for the hair, and elaborate gorgets for the breast; it served its turn as fetich and charm; was frequently used in the ceremonial jugglery of the mystic dance.[52]

Formerly four deer-skins was the price of a large conch-shell bead, about the length and thickness of a man's fore-finger; which they

[50] Schoolcraft, 1851, 1:67.
[51] Wintemberg, 1908, p. 63.
[52] Holmes, 1883, p. 188.

fixed to the crown of their head as an high ornament—so greatly they valued them.[53]

They frequently make of these shells, several sorts of Figures, in imitation of Gorges Crosses, Stars, or any other odd kind of Figure that their imagination suggests, these they wear about their Necks and Arms tied with a String; there are some of these Gorges, that will sell for three or four Buck Skins ready drest, whilst others are only valued and sold for one Doe Skin.[54]

COMMENTS ON UNUSUAL DEPTH OF BURIALS

The burials reported in this article were made at a depth of about six feet; those in Allen County, Indiana, were at a depth of ten feet; at least part of those in Hardin County, Ohio, reported by Greenman were at a depth of nearly twenty feet. Mr. Zimmerman, on whose farm they were found, claims one burial was twenty-two feet deep. Those in Randolph County, Indiana, were at a depth of twelve feet.

Were the bodies buried in the glacial drift so early that gravel accumulated over them to this depth, or were the graves dug nine to twenty feet deep? Although the Michigan artifacts are from a purely glacial sandbar, there is nothing to support the idea of the skeletons being of glacial antiquity; however, as the deposit had been formed partly by glacial action and perhaps later enlarged by the action of water, as sandbars are formed in a river, still another question is presented. If the graves were dug to a depth of nine to twenty or more feet, how was it accomplished? The gravel soil would not have been easy to dig into and hold, especially with primitive tools, because gravel is of such a nature that it continually slides into the excavation as the digging proceeds. Such excavations made with modern tools would be exceedingly dangerous today if the sides of the excavation were not properly cribbed. Did the maker of these shell artifacts use such cribbing? I know of no evidence to support this. It is probably true that the digging could have been done when the earth was frozen so hard that the gravel would not slide, but such a theory seems improbable, since the frost line is

[53] Adair, 1775, p. 170.
[54] Brickell, 1737, p. 337.

much too shallow to reach the depth of some of the reported graves.

There is the possibility that shallow graves were dug in the gravel, the bodies buried, and gravel from the same deposit piled on top. Owing to the fact that almost all finds of this type of shell artifact were the accidental discoveries of inexperienced individuals, the reports with the exception of the account of the Zimmerman site, do not answer these questions. Mr. Zimmerman stated that the outline of the individual grave was easily determined because the grave was of a darker soil than the surrounding gravel and was narrower at the bottom than at the top. This would indicate that the graves were dug, the bodies or skeletal remains dumped in, and the graves filled with a soil brought there from some other place.

SUMMARY ON SANDAL-SOLE ARTIFACTS AND ASSOCIATED ARTICLES

From the available information, the total of which is all too meager, it would appear that more sandal-sole shell artifacts and gravel burials have been unearthed in Ohio, and especially in Hardin and Mercer counties, than in any other part of the United States. At least one sandal sole has been found in Putnam County, Ohio, and some sandal soles have been found in Randolph and Allen counties, Indiana, and, possibly, in or near Richmond, Wayne County, Indiana, all six counties being within a radius of sixty miles of each other. Three and probably four have been discovered in Ontario, Canada. A surface find of one from Morgan County, Illinois, has been reported; another was taken from an artificial mound in Schuyler County, Illinois, one from Alabama, and, recently one from Lake Wawasee, Kosciusko County, Indiana, in addition to those described in this article from Branch County, Michigan (Map 1). Most have been in gravel deposits, although those reported from Canada and Illinois were not. Practically all were associated with human bones, copper implements, ashes, charcoal, shell beads, and other shell artifacts. With some were stone artifacts, but there was a notable scarcity of pottery.

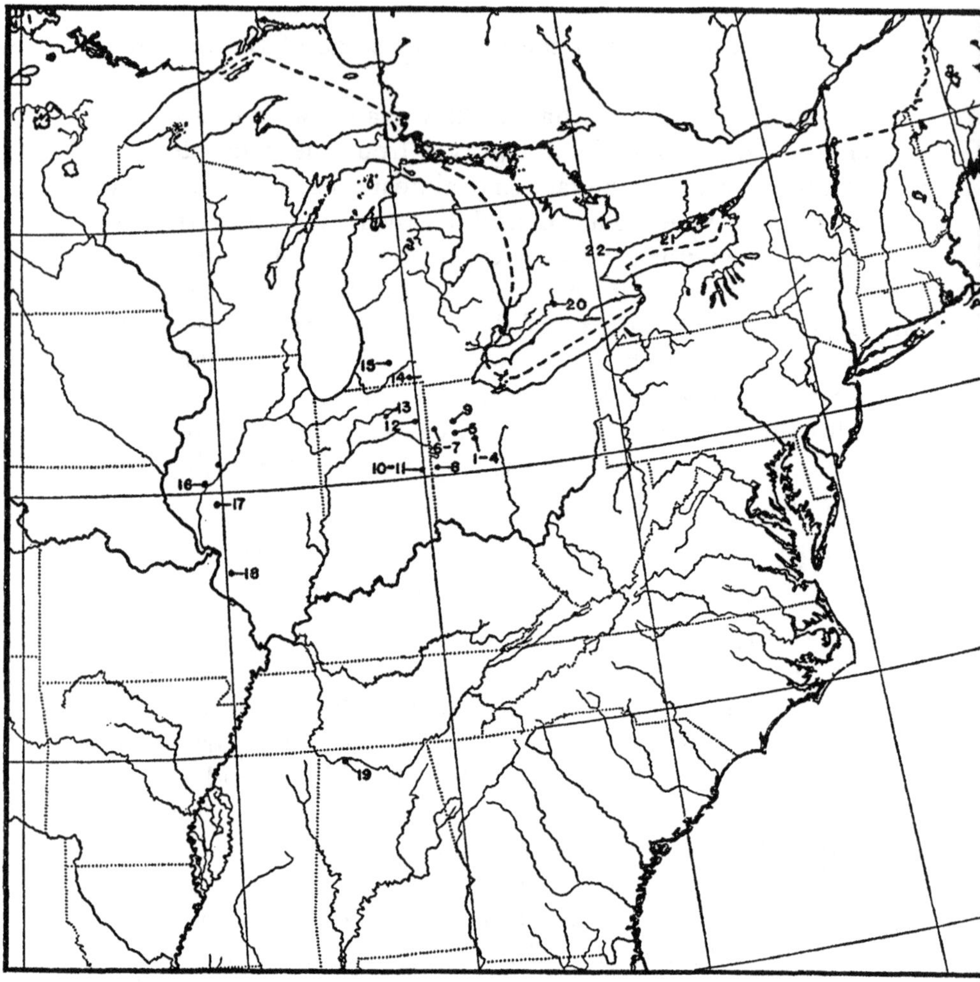

MAP 1. Sites attributed to the Glacial Kame culture.

(1) Ridgeway site, Hardin County, Ohio. (2) Spitzer site, Hardin County, Ohio. (3) Stiner site, Hardin County, Ohio. (4) Zimmerman site, Hardin County, Ohio. (5) Snyder site Auglaize County, Ohio. (6) Sharpsburg site, Mercer County, Ohio. (7) Fox-Rammel sites Mercer County, Ohio. (8) Unnamed site, Darke County, Ohio. (9) Unnamed site, Putman County, Ohio. (10) Lynn site, Randolph County, Indiana. (11) Mulen site, Randolph County Indiana. (12) Unnamed site, Allen County, Indiana. (13) Cedar Point site, Kosciusko County Indiana. (14) Burch site, Branch County, Michigan. (15) Harrison site, Kalamazoo County Michigan. (16) Dixon mound, Sugar Creek, Schuyler County, Illinois. (17) Unnamed site Morgan County, Illinois. (18) Cahokia Mound, St. Clair-Madison counties, Illinois. (19) Georgetown Landing, Colbert County, Alabama. (20) Blackfriar's Bridge site, Middlesex County, Ontario. (21) Picton site, Prince Edward County, Ontario. (22) Weston site, York County, Ontario.

In all, not more than one hundred sandal soles, including a few known duplications, can be accounted for in the possession of museums and collectors.

Because this form of shell artifacts has such definite geographic boundaries (with the exception of a very few finds), it is of more than ordinary interest to the archaeologist.

There can be no doubt that the complex represented and characterized by the list of traits mentioned above exists to a greater or lesser extent in Ohio, Indiana, Ontario, Michigan, Alabama, and Illinois. Although it is true that well-known authorities have suggested that this is "Glacial Kame" culture, the designation is not always accurate, for such artifacts have been reported from artificial mounds and graves. This, possibly, can be accounted for by migration, intermarriage, and other usual means of cultural diffusion.

From what can be learned there has never been any systematic investigation by archaeologists of this type of burial, of the shell and copper artifacts with it, and of the history of the people who made and used the artifacts. This was observed by Moorehead in 1897, when he stated that no archaeologist seemed to have paid attention to glacial kame and gravel knoll burials.[55] This may be accounted for by the fact that these articles are scarce, and few gravel deposits yield such material to the excavator. Artificial mounds, because of their limited number, can be excavated systematically, but the most enthusiastic scientist could hardly be expected to work numberless gravel pits and kames.

CONCLUSION

Although a comparison of the Red Ochre Phase, as outlined by Cole and Deuel,[56] makes it appear that between the Red Ochre Phase and that characterized by the shell artifacts from Michigan, there are many traits in common, such as flexed burials, red ochre associated with the burials, red ochre on the artifacts, spherical beads, copper awl (square section), shell

[55] Moorehead, 1897, p. 261.

[56] Cole and Deuel, 1937.

disk gorgets (although the perforations in the Illinois finds are lacking), shell gorgets, charcoal, and ashes, it must not be overlooked that there are also a great many differences. For instance, the mounds in Illinois are reported to be artificial. In Illinois flint objects were discovered as well as pieces of antler, galena, polished hematite, copper tubing, a celt, deer bones, bundle burials, cremated remains, and, possibly, potsherds. None of these was in the Michigan gravel deposit.

It must be remembered, however, that the Michigan find was made by farmers who were not versed in archaeology and that the remainder of the deposit has never been explored. A thorough excavation might reveal stone artifacts or other red ochre traits, such as were discovered in Illinois.

Although stone axes, flint arrow points, slate implements, tubular slate pipes, banner stones, celts of slate, and a platform pipe are reported as having been associated with sandal-sole gorgets, none was taken with the Michigan artifacts. The platform pipe found with two sandal-sole shell gorgets and a shell disk gorget at a depth of ten feet in a gravel pit in Allen County, Indiana, has already been mentioned. This resembles pipes from Hopewellian mounds.

The Adena Aspect is said to be characterized generally by conical mounds, log tombs, bark prepared graves, subfloor burials, important central graves, pottery, tubular tobacco pipes, stone gorgets, copper bracelets, projectile points, mica, and mostly uncremated burials,[57] red ochre is also present occasionally. None of these traits is found with the Michigan artifacts with the exception of the copper ornaments, red ochre, and the uncremated skeletons (Table I).

The Hopewellian Phase is said to be characterized generally by log tombs, well-prepared burial floors of stone or clay, cremation of the dead, pottery, copper plates and bracelets, pearls used for beads, obsidian, effigy platform pipes, ear spools of clay, cut and perforated human and animal jaws, and slate gorgets.[58]

[57] Shetrone, 1931, pp. 167–69.

[58] *Ibid.*, pp. 185–222.

I know of no record of log tombs in gravel deposits. It would have been less work to construct the tombs and then cover them with earth, as was done in both Adena and Hopewellian, than to dig a hole of the necessary size and depth in crumbly gravel, to build the tomb, and then to cover it with gravel.

Although many traits of the Hopewellian Phase are lacking in the Michigan find, and although artifacts of the Hopewellian Phase have been found in artificial mounds and most of the sandal-sole type of shell gorgets in natural gravel deposits, more artifacts similar to those associated with this special type of shell artifact have been associated with Hopewellian than with any other division, and on the basis of the artifacts the complex represented by the sandal-sole shell gorgets and related artifacts resembles the Hopewellian more nearly than it does any other, even though there are many differences. Hopewellian remains have been reported in western Michigan, and also near Tecumseh, Lenawee County, Michigan.[59]

The finding of Lake Superior copper objects, gorgets made from ocean shells, and a few ivory artifacts indicates that an extensive commerce was carried on by their users. This is mentioned because so little is known of the artifacts and burials discussed in this article that each and every trait and circumstance becomes important. No definite conclusions can be made from the few facts disclosed regarding the complex represented by the shell and copper artifacts generally in gravel deposits.

[59] Shetrone, 1931, pp. 280–81.

TABLE I

Trait List for Eleven Glacial Kame Sites

		Burch	Sharps-burg	Fox-Rammel	Ridge-way	Zimmer-man	Sugar Creek	Mulen	Cedar Point	Allen County	Black-friars	Picton
Traits at one site only	Broken and burned rock fireplace	...	...	...	...	...	...	...	x	...	...	...
	Small Woodland Plain vessels	...	...	...	...	x	...	...	...	...	...	...
	Stone axe or celt	...	...	...	x	...	...	...	...	...	...	...
	Bell-shaped pestle	...	...	...	...	x	...	...	...	...	...	...
	Slate implement	...	...	...	x	...	...	...	...	...	...	...
	Banded slate bead	...	...	...	...	x	...	...	...	...	...	...
	Black slate celt	...	...	...	...	...	...	x	...	...	...	...
	Engraved bone bird head	...	...	...	...	x	...	...	...	...	...	...
	Perforated elk tooth	...	...	...	...	x	...	...	...	...	...	...
	Deer bones and horns	...	...	...	x	...	...	...	...	...	...	...
	Bone beads	...	...	...	x	...	...	...	...	...	...	...
	Deer bone awls	...	...	...	x	...	...	...	...	...	...	...
	Deer antler handle	...	...	...	...	...	x	...	...	...	...	...
	Turtle shell rattle	...	...	...	...	...	x	...	...	...	...	...
	Bird buried with skeleton	...	...	...	x	...	...	...	...	...	...	...
	Burials without skulls	...	...	...	x	...	...	...	...	...	...	...
	Double burial, male and female	...	...	x	...	...	...	...	...	...	...	...
	Multiple bundle burial ossuary	...	...	x	...	...	...	...	...	...	...	...
	Perforated skull	...	...	x	...	...	...	...	...	...	...	...
	Village (?) burials	...	...	...	...	...	...	...	x	...	...	...
	Copper stains on burial	...	...	...	...	...	...	...	x	...	...	...
	Copper gouge	...	...	...	...	...	...	...	...	...	...	x
	Copper bar gorget	x	...	...	...	...	...	...	...	...	...	...
	Copper plate-punctated	...	...	...	x	...	...	...	...	...	...	...
	Perforated clam shell	...	...	...	...	x	...	...	...	...	...	...
	Clam shell filled with red paint	...	...	...	x	...	...	...	...	...	...	...
	Beads around neck	...	...	...	x	...	...	...	...	...	...	...
	Imitation cut animal jaw of shell	...	...	...	x	...	...	...	...	...	...	...
	Large string of shell beads	...	...	...	x	...	...	...	...	...	...	...
	Conch shell beads	...	...	...	x	...	...	...	...	...	...	...
	Heart-shaped shell pendant	...	...	...	...	...	...	...	...	...	x	...
	Shell gorget, one perforation	...	...	...	...	...	...	...	...	x	...	...

Traits at two sites	Flint arrowpoints	...	...	...	x	x	...	...	...	...	...	...
	Slate birdstone	...	...	...	x	Harrison site			...	...	...	...
	Stone platform pipe	...	...	...	...	...	x	...	...	x	...	...
	Tubular stone pipe	...	...	...	...	x	...	x	...	...	...	...
	Red paint with skeletons	x	...	...	...	...	...	...	...	...	...	x
	Dog burial with skeletons	...	...	...	x	...	...	...	x	...	...	...
	Burial covered with bark	...	...	x	...	...	...	...	...	...	...	x
	Charred human bones, cremation (?)	...	...	...	x	...	...	...	...	...	...	x
	Mound burial (?)	...	x	...	...	...	x	...	...	...	...	...
	Burial face down	...	...	...	x	x	...	...	...	...	...	...
	Copper axe	...	x	...	...	...	...	...	...	...	...	x
	Large shell beads	...	...	...	x	...	...	x	...	...	...	...
	Cylindrical shell beads	...	...	...	...	...	...	...	...	...	x	x
	Shell beads	...	x	...	...	x	...	...	...	...	...	...
	Conch shell containers	...	...	...	...	x	...	x	...	...	...	...
	Irregular shell gorgets	x	...	...	...	...	x	...	...	...	...	...
	Engraved sandal-sole gorgets	...	...	...	...	x	...	x	...	...	...	...
More than two sites	Sandal-sole gorget on head	...	...	...	x	...	x	x	...	...	...	...
	Extended burials	...	...	x	x	...	x	...	...	...	...	x
	Copper awl	x(1)	...	...	...	...	x(2)	...	...	...	...	x
	Charcoal and ashes	x	...	x	x	x	...	...	x	...	...	...
	Flexed burial	x(10?)	...	x	x	x	...	...	x	...	...	...
	Deep burial in gravel kame	x	...	x	x	x	...	x	...	x	...	...
	Shell disk beads	x	...	x	...	x	...	x	...	...	x	x
	Oblong shell gorgets	x(2)	...	x(2)	x(6)	x	...	x(1)	...	x(1)	...	...
	Copper beads	x(17)	...	x	x	x(144)	x	...	...	...	...	x
	Three-hole disk gorget	x(3)	...	x(1)	x(1)	...	...	x(3)	x(8)	...	x(5)	x(1)
	Sandal-sole shell gorget	x(5)	x(20)	x(10)	x(3)	x(14)	x(1)	x(3)	x(1)	x(2)	x(1)	x(1)
	Total traits (61)	12	4	13	28	19	10	11	8	5	5	12

BIBLIOGRAPHY

ADAIR, JAMES

1775 History of the American Indians. London: Printed for E. and C. Dilly.

BLACK, GLENN A.

1934 Archaeological Survey of Dearborn and Ohio Counties. Ind. Hist Bull., XI, No. 7.

BRICKELL, JOHN

1737 The Natural History of North Carolina. Dublin: Printed by J. Carson for the author.

COLE, FAY-COOPER, and THORNE DEUEL

1937 Rediscovering Illinois; Archaeological Explorations in and Around Fulton County. Chicago: Univ. Chicago Press.

FAIRBANKS, CHARLES H.

1942 The Taxonomic Position of Stallings's Island, Georgia. Amer. Antiq., No. 3: 223–31.

FUNKHOUSER, WILLIAM D., and WILLIAM S. WEBB

1937 The Chilton Site in Henry County, Kentucky. Univ. Kentucky Rept. Archaeol. and Anthropol., III, No. 5.

GREENMAN, EMERSON F.

1931 Plans for the Coming Field Season. Mus. Echoes, 4, No. 8.

GRIFFIN, JAMES B.

1943 The Fort Ancient Aspect: Its Cultural and Chronological Position in Mississippi Valley Archaeology. Ann Arbor: Univ. Michigan Press.

1946 Cultural Change and Continuity in Eastern United States Archaeology. *In* Papers Peabody Foundation for Archaeol., 3: 37–96.

HAAG, WILLIAM G.

1942*a* A Description and Analysis of the Pickwick Pottery. *In* Webb and DeJarnette, pp. 509–27.

1942*b* Early Horizons in the Southeast. Amer. Antiq., VII, No. 3: 209–22.

HOLMES, WILLIAM H.

1883 Art in Shell of the Ancient Americans. Second Ann. Rept. Bur. Amer. Ethnol., pp. 185–267.

JACKSON, ALVIN T.

1941 Pendants and Their Uses. Bull. Texas Archeol. and Paleontol. Soc., 13: 9–46.

LANGFORD, GEORGE

1927 The Fisher Mound Group, Successive Aboriginal Occupations near the Mouth of the Illinois River. Amer. Anthropol., 29: 152–206.

Leverett, Frank, and Frank B. Taylor
1915 The Pleistocene of Indiana and Michigan and the History of the Great Lakes. Monogr. U. S. Geol. Surv., Vol. LIII.

Lilly, Eli
1942 A Cedar Point "Glacial Kame" Burial. Proc. Ind. Acad. Sci., 51: 31–34.

Mason, Otis T.
1881 Abstracts of the Smithsonian Correspondence Relative to Aboriginal Remains in the United States. Ann. Rept. Smithson. Instit. for 1880, pp. 441–48.

McAllister, J. Gilbert
1932 The Archaeology of Greene County. Ind. Hist. Bull., X, No. 5.

Mills, William C.
1922 Exploration of the Mound City Group. Certain Mounds and Village Sites in Ohio. Columbus: F. J. Heer. 3, Pt. 4.

Montgomery, Henry
1906 Remains of Prehistoric Man in the Dakotas. Amer. Anthropol., 8, No. 4: 640–51.

Moore, Clarence B.
1893 Certain Shell Heaps of the St. John's River, Florida, Hitherto Unexplored. Amer. Nat., XXVII: 708–23.

Moorehead, Warren K.
1895 [Ed.] Archaeologist, III, No. 4: 146–47.
1897 Report of Field Work. Ohio Archaeol. and Hist. Publ., V: 165–275.
1899 Report of Field Work. *Ibid.*, VII: 110–205.
1900 Prehistoric Implements. Cincinnati: The Robert Clarke Co.
1909 A Study of Primitive Culture in Ohio. *In* Putnam Anniversary Volume. New York: G. E. Stechert. Pp. 137–51.
1910 The Stone Age in North America. New York: Houghton Mifflin Co. 2 vols.
1917 Stone Ornaments of the American Indian. Andover: Andover Press.
1922*a* A Report on the Archaeology of Maine. Andover: Andover Press.
1922*b* The Hopewell Mound Group of Ohio. Field Mus. Nat. Hist., Anthropol. Ser., 6, No. 5.

Morgan, Richard G. and H. Holmes Ellis
1943 The Fairport Harbor Site. Ohio State Archaeol. and Hist. Quart., 52, No. 1: 1–60.

Parker, Arthur C.
1922 The Archaeological History of New York. N. Y. State Mus. Bull., Nos. 235–36.

Perkins, George H.
1874 On an Ancient Burial-Ground in Swanton, Vt. Proc. Amer. Assn. Adv. Sci., 22, Pt. B: 77–100.

Putnam, Frederick W.
1884 Sixteenth and Seventeenth Ann. Rept. Peabody Mus. Amer. Archaeol. and Ethnol.

Quimby, George I., Jr.
1941 The Goodall Focus: An Analysis of Ten Hopewellian Components in Michigan and Indiana. Prehistory Research Ser., Indiana Hist. Soc., Vol. II, No. 2.

Ritchie, William A.
1938*a* New Archaeological Discoveries at Brewerton, New York. Bull. Rochester Mus. Arts. and Sci., Dec., 1938.
1938*b* A Perspective of Northeastern Archaeology. Amer. Antiq., IV, No. 2: 94–113.
1940 Two Prehistoric Village Sites at Brewerton, New York. Res. Records Rochester Mus. Arts and Sci., No. 5.

Schoolcraft, Henry R.
1851–57. Historical and Statistical Information, Respecting the History, Condition and Prospects of the Indian Tribes of the United States: Collected and Prepared under the Direction of the Bureau of Indian Affairs. Philadelphia: Lippincott, Grambo and Company. 6 pts.

Shetrone, Henry C.
1920 The Culture Problem in Ohio Archaeology. Amer. Anthropol., 22 No. 2: 145–72.
1931 The Mound Builders. New York: D. Appleton and Company.

Snodgrass, Jesse
1894 Carved Shell. Archaeologist, II, No. 4: 114–15.

Strong, William D.
1940 From History to Prehistory in the Northern Great Plains. *In* Essays in Historical Anthropology of North America. Smithson. Misc. Coll., 100: 353–94.

Webb, William S.
1939 An Archaeological Survey of Wheeler Basin on the Tennessee River in Northern Alabama. Bur. Amer. Ethnol. Bull., 122.

Webb, William S., and David I. DeJarnette
1942 An Archaeological Survey of Pickwick Basin in the Adjacent Portions of the States of Alabama, Mississippi and Tennessee. Bur. Amer. Ethnol. Bull., 129.

Webb, William S., and William G. Haag
1939 The Chiggerville Site. Univ. Kentucky Repts. in Anthropol. Vol. IV, No. 1.

West, George A.
1934 Tobacco, Pipes and Smoking Customs of the American Indians. Bull. Public Mus. Milwaukee, Vol. XVII.

WHITTLESEY, CHARLES, and MATTHEW C. READ
1877 Antiquities of Ohio, Ohio Centennial Rept. Columbus: Nevins and Myers. Pp. 81–139.

WINTEMBERG, WILLIAM J.
1908 The Use of Shells by the Ontario Indians. Ann. Archaeol. Rept., 1907, Appendix to Rept. Minister of Educ., Ontario, pp. 38–90.
1928 Artifacts from Ancient Graves and Mounds in Ontario. Trans. Royal Soc. Canada, Third Ser., XXII, Sec. II: 175–202.

APPENDIX

AN INTERPRETATION OF THE GLACIAL KAME CULTURE

By James B. Griffin

It is clear that the data gathered together by Cunningham do not describe a unit of aboriginal life which can be called a "culture." They are material remains of a burial complex. Although this complex does contain objects and concepts derived from a larger cultural whole, it would be presumptuous to attempt any definition of the Glacial Kame "culture" or to assign it to specific classificatory units. In addition to the fact that this is a burial complex, it should be remembered that all of the sites and finds have been recovered by individuals who were not only not archaeologists but in many cases by those who had no interest in archaeology. Thus, even the apparent random distribution of artifact types perhaps inherent in mortuary practices in this area[1] is accentuated by the absence of reliable information regarding the sites and the lack of adequate descriptions of the artifacts. The trait list which has been prepared for some of the sites is thus inadequate in many respects, but it does serve to objectify a number of impressions regarding this division of northern Woodland culture.

More than half of the sixty-one traits listed are present at only one site, and about 25 per cent are found at only two sites. Only one trait, the sandal-sole gorget, is at all eleven sites. The next most common trait is the three-hole gorget, which is reported at seven sites. Furthermore, not a single site has even a majority of the total number of traits listed for the eleven sites. Most of the sites have only one-fifth or less of the total traits. What justification then is there for the grouping of these sites into any kind of a cultural unit? The presence of the distinctive sandal-sole gorget is the "diagnostic" trait which implies a cultural connection (of unknown intensity) sufficient to warrant

[1] Quimby, 1941, p. 138; Wintemberg, 1928, p. 195.

this unit. This recognition is aided and abetted by the lack of a trait or group of traits which would clearly allocate these sites to other recognized burial complexes or culture units. The three-hole gorget, oblong or rectangular shell gorget, and a general emphasis on shell artifacts as mortuary furniture is a fairly constant accompanying feature. Nineteen of the sixty-one traits are referable to the use of shell. Also of considerable importance is the presence of a few copper beads, awls, axes, gouges, or plates. The placement of the dead in the gravel deposits sometimes at a considerable depth is an outstanding feature of some but not all of the sites which are referable to this burial complex.

An attempt to allocate this complex to any cultural division or chronological period is handicapped by the factors mentioned above and by the scarcity of archaeological data for the area in which the majority of the sites are situated. The most recent systematic work was done by Black in the Fort Wayne–South Bend area during the summers of 1936 and 1937. This was primarily an attempt to identify the archaeological culture of the various historic tribes of that area. This was not accomplished, but some additional information on the prehistoric groups in the area helps to round out the general picture and gives some suggestions as to the possible place of the Glacial Kame complex. The presence of the Hopewellian Phase along the east side of Lake Michigan was recognized,[2] but a comparative statement has only recently been made available.[3] Equally significant was the discovery of the presence of Oneota and Fisher Focus influence in the southwest corner of Michigan and the north-central part of Indiana.[4] In the southeastern part of Michigan, Hopewell artifacts are associated with predominantly Woodland sites and the succeeding cultural complex begins to take on an Iroquoian cast.[5] This situation is also present in northern Ohio.[6]

[2] Shetrone, 1931, pp. 247, 280.

[3] Quimby, 1941, p. 138.

[4] Griffin, 1943, p. 282.

[5] The Gibraltar site. Museum of Anthropology, University of Michigan.

[6] Greenman, 1931, p. 42; also a forthcoming report by Greenman on the Esch mounds and Heimberger village site; with a section on pottery by J. B. Griffin.

The Ceramic Repository for the Eastern United States at the University of Michigan has a small collection of Woodland sherds from Mercer County, Ohio, which are culturally closest to pottery from the late Woodland occupation of central[7] and northern Indiana.

To a marked extent these cultural manifestations have not been found in what might be called the central area of the Glacial Kame finds. This presents the possibility that the burial complex under discussion represents the funeral gifts and burial customs of a group of people who occupied the area to the exclusion of other known cultural units. There is no suggestion in the artifact content of a migratory movement into the area nor is there any clear suggestion of a movement out of the area. The artifacts and burials do, however, give evidence from the standpoint of comparative typology as to the cultural and chronological position of this complex. Speaking generally, neither copper nor ocean shell artifacts play a particularly prominent place in the early levels of Eastern United States archaeology.[8] It is not until the early Woodland period of the Adena culture in the central Ohio drainage basin that copper is prominent, and it is not until Hopewell times that there is a marked use of ocean shell with an elaborated copper artifact complex. In the Illinois Valley, the Red Ochre sites have shell artifacts somewhat resembling the sandal-sole gorget and the circular gorget, with copper gorgets, beads, and awls.[9] This burial complex is believed to be earlier than Illinois Valley Hopewellian in which are shell and copper specimens comparable to those of the Ohio Aspect.

Also to be considered in this discussion are the copper axes, copper beads, large ovoid shell pendants, and the three-hole disk pendants from the Fisher site.[10] Unfortunately, for various reasons, a definitive picture of the Fisher Focus, following

[7] Griffin, 1943, pp. 261–67.

[8] Haag, 1942*b*; Fairbanks, 1942; Webb and DeJarnette, 1942; Ritchie, 1940, p. 44.

[9] Cole and Deuel, 1937, Fig. 19.

[10] Langford, 1927, Pls. XV and XVI.

Langford's excellent earlier papers, has not appeared. Hence, there is some hesitation in the correct allocation of these artifacts to each other and to the rest of the cultural material at the Fisher site. The three-hole gorgets, although similar to those in the Glacial Kame sites, are not identical because of the markedly increased size of the central hole. This feature is also present in the three-hole gorgets of the Fort Ancient Aspect and other late cultural groups in the Mississippi Valley.[11]

The tubular pipes do not have the shapes distinctive of Adena culture. Various types of tubular pipes are widely distributed in both Americas.[12] The specimen from the Mulen site is a simple type. Similar specimens are known from the west coast[13] to New York[14] and to the shell mounds of northern Alabama.[15] The specimen from the Zimmerman site has a bulbous mouthpiece and strongly resembles tubular pipes of this shape also found from the west coast[16] to the Atlantic.[17] Specimens from North Dakota[18] are apparently connected with the Arvilla Focus of Wilford.[19]

The straight-based platform pipe has two cross-hatched areas near one end[20] which resemble the design placed on a platform pipe from Porter County, Indiana.[21] These two pipes also resemble each other in having flat bases and a similarly shaped bowl. The outline of the platform is, however, somewhat different, and the Porter County specimen has a ridge above the stem perforation which is also on platform pipes of the "Intrusive Mound Culture."[22] It is unfortunate that the platform pipe from the Sugar Creek site is not available for comparison.

[11] Griffin, 1943, p. 283.
[12] West, 1934.
[13] *Ibid.*, Pl. 13, Fig. 9.
[14] Parker, 1922, Pl. 21.
[15] Webb and DeJarnette, 1942, Pl. 37, Fig. 2; Pl. 94, Fig. 1.
[16] West, 1934, Pl. 17, Fig. 6.
[17] Moorehead, 1922*a*, Figs. 118 and 119.
[18] Montgomery, 1906, Pl. XXXIII.
[19] Strong, 1940, p. 386.
[20] West, 1934, Pl. 52, Fig. 1.
[21] McAllister, 1932, Pl. 23.
[22] Mills, 1922, Figs. 83 and 90.

The bird stones belong to the polished slate ceremonial forms of the Great Lakes and northeastern part of the country. They are not commonly associated with other material in burials from the Middle West[23] but are from the New England area and New York.[24] In the famous Swanton graves a bird stone[25] identical typologically with that from the Hopewell Mound and from the Point Peninsula Oberlander site[26] was associated with copper implements, tubular pipes (some of these pipes are very similar to the specimen from the Zimmerman site), ocean shell beads, and triangular points of Point Peninsula shape.[27] Shell gorgets identical in shape with those illustrated in Plate II are described by Parker from Livingston County, New York.[28] Unfortunately, little is known of their cultural association.

It is difficult to do much with burial practices as cultural indicators, especially when there are so many different types of body disposition as are described from the Glacial Kame sites. That this burial complex is not usual in artificial mounds is a reflection of its geographical position along the northern margin of mound building as much as it is of its chronological position.

The comparative section in Cunningham's paper and the additional data provided in this discussion have served to emphasize that the Glacial Kame complex has the majority of its related associations in the northeastern part of the country and that specific traits and trait associations are in numerous Woodland cultural divisions, including the Adena-Hopewellian.[29] Since a satisfactory cultural assignment is difficult, a placement within the Hopewellian Phase is probably not too accurate. In view of certain specific analogies with the Hopewellian culture, this complex could hardly have occurred earlier than Hopewell. In southern Canada there is not only no trace of white contact in this burial complex, but there is also no evidence of Iroquoian

[23] Moorehead, 1922*b*, Fig. 34.

[24] Parker, 1922, pp. 90–92.

[25] Moorehead, 1922*a*, Fig. 120c.

[26] Ritchie, 1938*a*, Pl. 1cc.

[27] Perkins, 1874, p. 98.

[28] *In* Moorehead, 1917, p. 209.

[29] Morgan and Ellis, 1943, p. 61.

artifacts, which suggests that the Glacial Kame sites in this area are at least as early as 1400 to 1500. This is also the conclusion implicit in Wintemberg's paper on this manifestation in Canada[30] and the same or a greater degree of antiquity is attributed to the related culture groups in New York and New England.[31] In the Michigan–Indiana–Ohio area Hopewellian is generally attributed to a date around 1200.[32] In Lilly's recent paper[33] on the occurrence of a sandal-sole gorget in northern Indiana, he has pointed out the possible interpretations of the presence of a half-penny coin of the period between 1790–1810 with a burial. No other data regarding this burial is known (it cannot be proved that the coin was deposited with the skeleton) and in view of the absence of similar indication of a late date with other Glacial Kame burials and because of the considerably earlier age usually attributed to the artifacts of the Glacial Kame complex, it is doubtful that Lilly's suggestion of a late date for the gorget can be substantiated. The physical type of the burials is not only historic in the area but is also one of the oldest in the Middle West, hence the physical type is hardly an accurate guide to the age of the burials.

The Glacial Kame artifacts suggest that they belong to a Woodland burial complex toward the close of the Hopewellian or Middle Woodland period and near the beginning of the period of the spread of Middle Mississippi.

[30] Wintemberg, 1928.

[31] Ritchie, 1938*a* and 1938*b*.

[32] Griffin, 1946.

[33] Lilly, 1942.

PLATE I

Specimens from the Burch Site, Branch County; Michigan.

Fig. 1. Shell disk beads.

Fig. 2. Small string of copper beads.

Fig. 3. Copper gorget with two punched holes.

Fig. 4. Copper awl with square cross section.

Figs. 5–7. Three shell gorgets with one central and two marginal perforations.

Photographs by Richard M. Snodgrasse.

PLATE I

Fig. 1

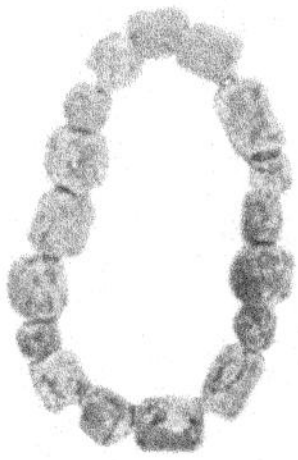

Fig. 2

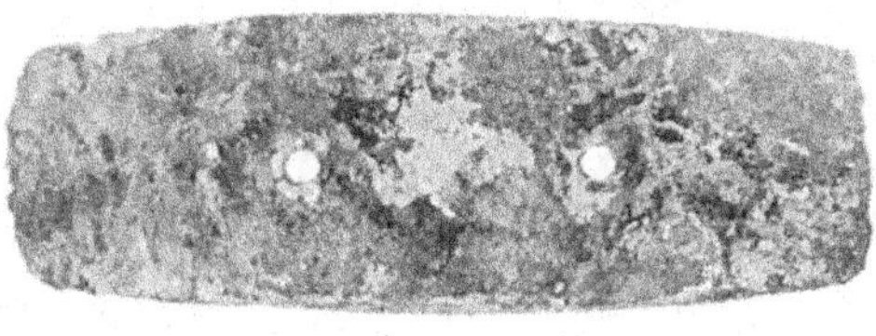

Fig. 3

Fig. 4

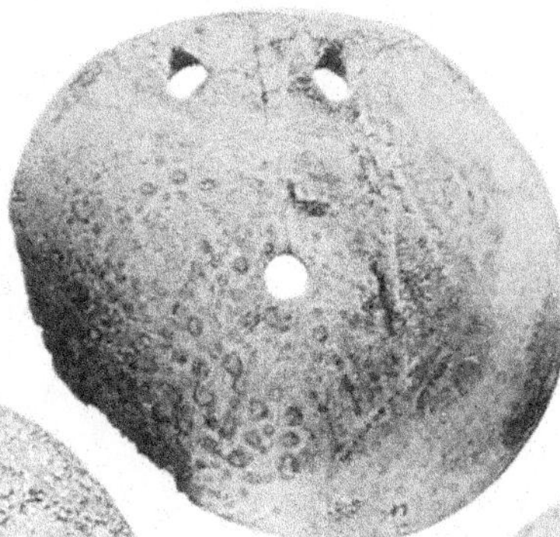

Fig. 6

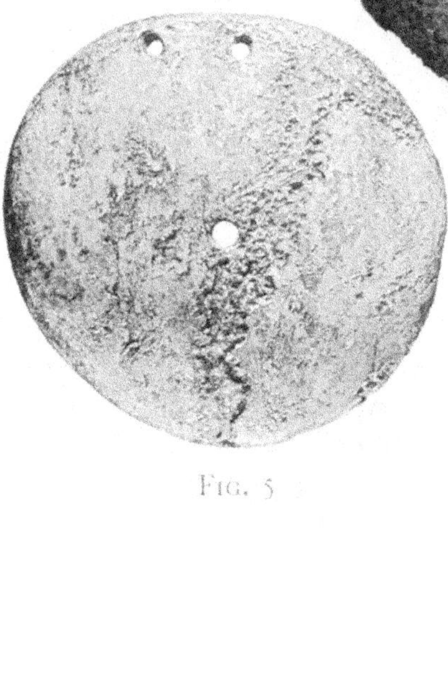

Fig. 5

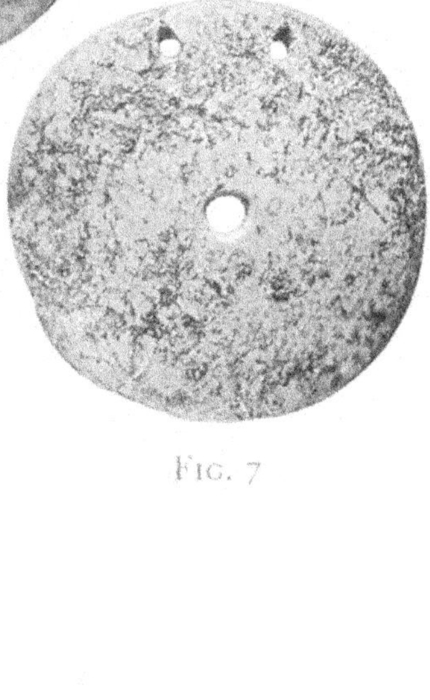

Fig. 7

PLATE II

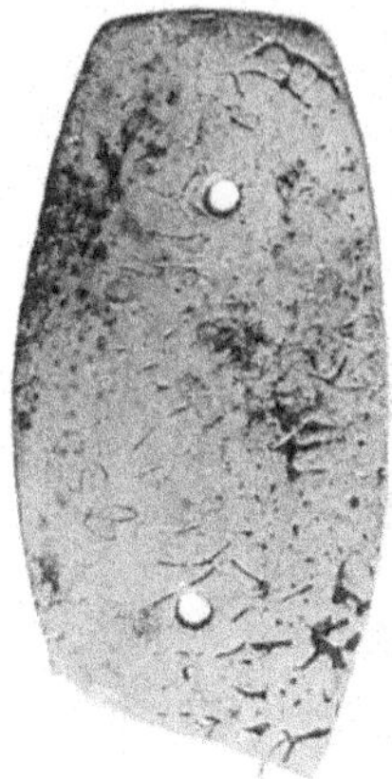

Fig. 1

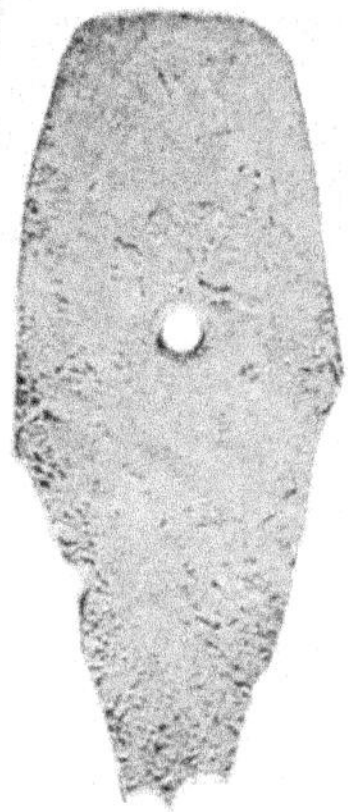

Fig. 2

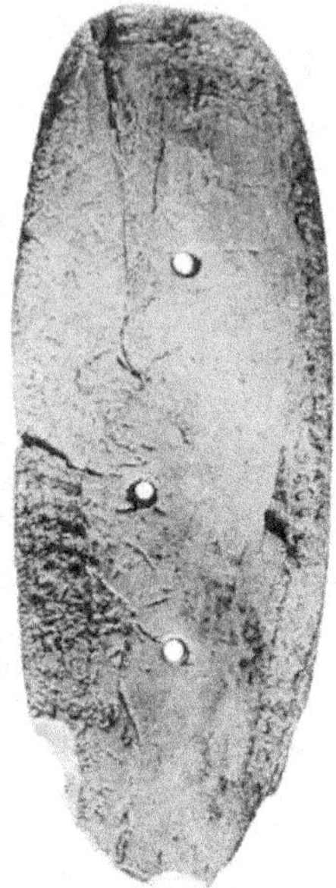

Fig. 3

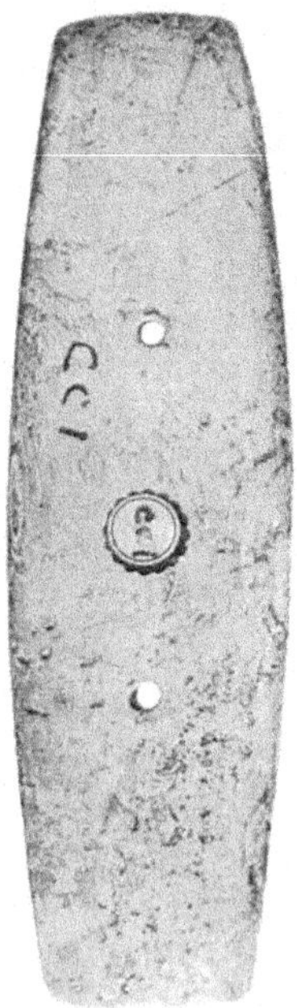

Fig. 4

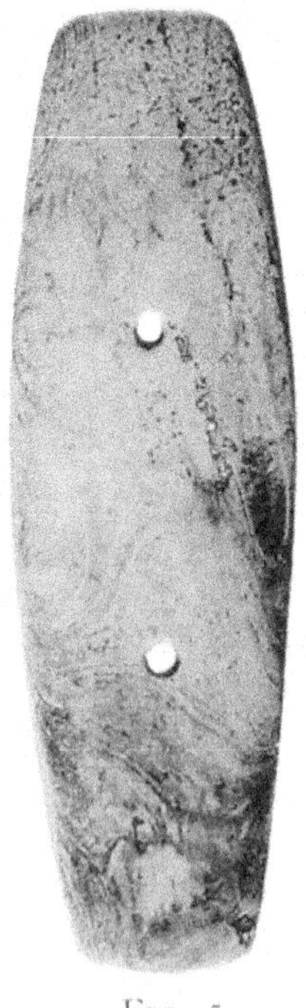

Fig. 5

PLATE II

FIGS. 1–3. Broken shell gorgets from the Burch site, Branch County, Michigan. The fragment in Figure 3 is five and one-half inches long.

FIGS. 4–5. Two oblong gorgets from the Burch site. The gorget illustrated in Figure 5 is six and one-half inches long. Photographs by Richard M. Snodgrasse.

PLATE III

Figs. 1–5. Five sandal-sole gorgets from the Burch site, Branch County, Michigan. Photograph by Richard M. Snodgrasse.

Figs. 6–7. Two shell gorgets of unusual shape from the Burch site: concave surface (Fig. 6) and convex surface (Fig. 7). Photograph by Glenn A. Black.

PLATE III

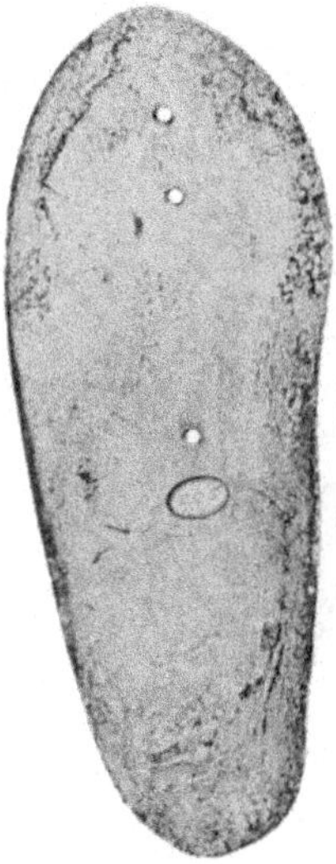

Fig. 1

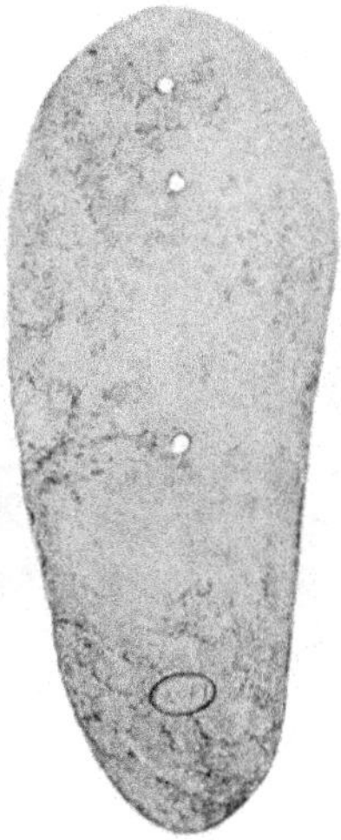

Fig. 2

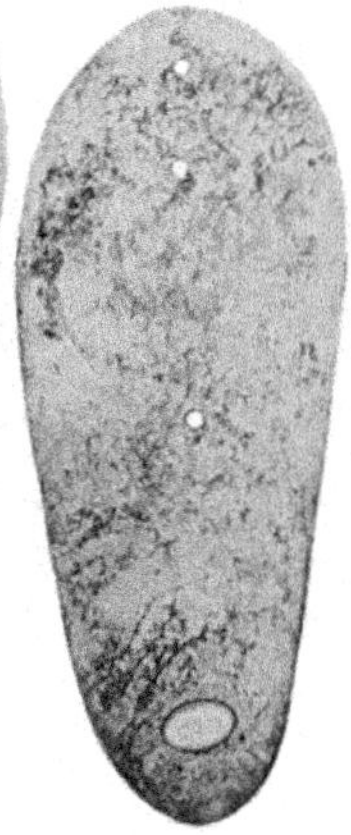

Fig. 3

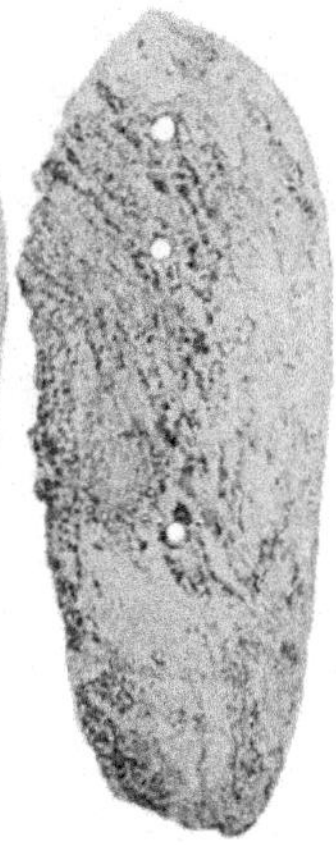

Fig. 4

Fig. 5

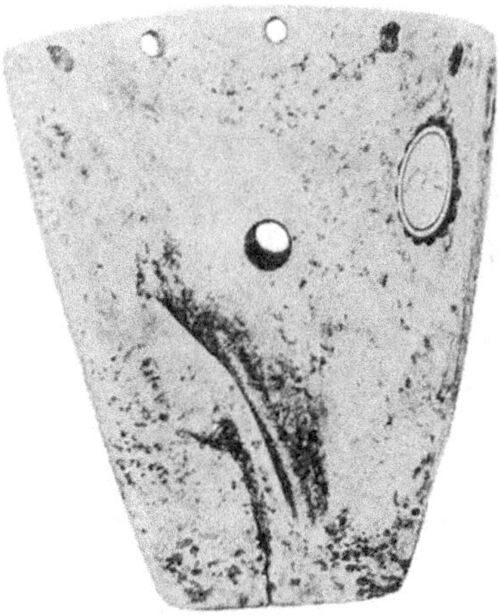

Fig. 6

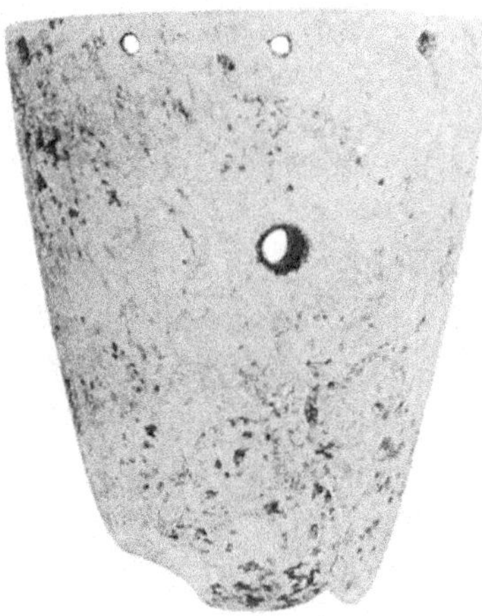

Fig. 7

PLATE IV

FIG. 1

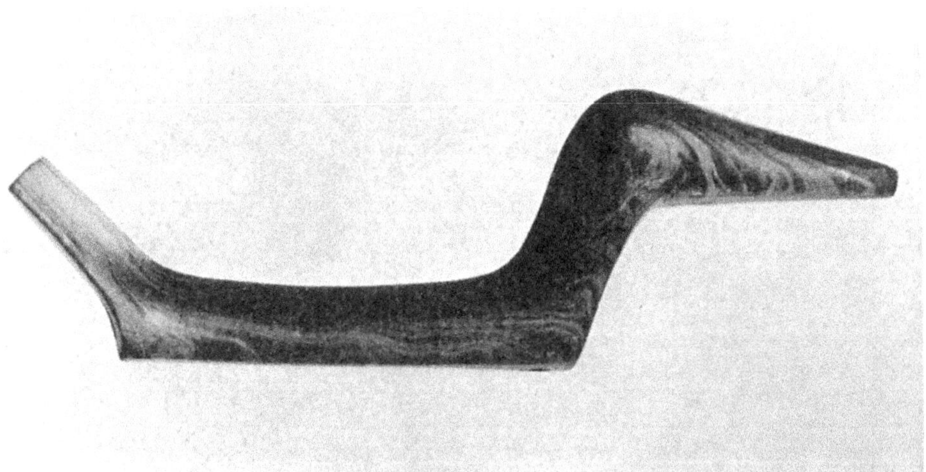

FIG. 2

PLATE IV

FIG. 1. Slate birdstone from the Harrison site, Kalamazoo County, Michigan. Milwaukee Public Museum photograph.

FIG. 2. Banded slate birdstone from a gravel pit burial two and one-half miles west of Lynn, Randolph County, Indiana. Red ochre, several copper beads, and two notched projectile points were associated with the burial. Ohio State Museum photograph.

PLATE V

Broken sandal-sole gorget with crack-lacing holes from Picton, Ontario. In the National Museum of Canada.

PLATE V

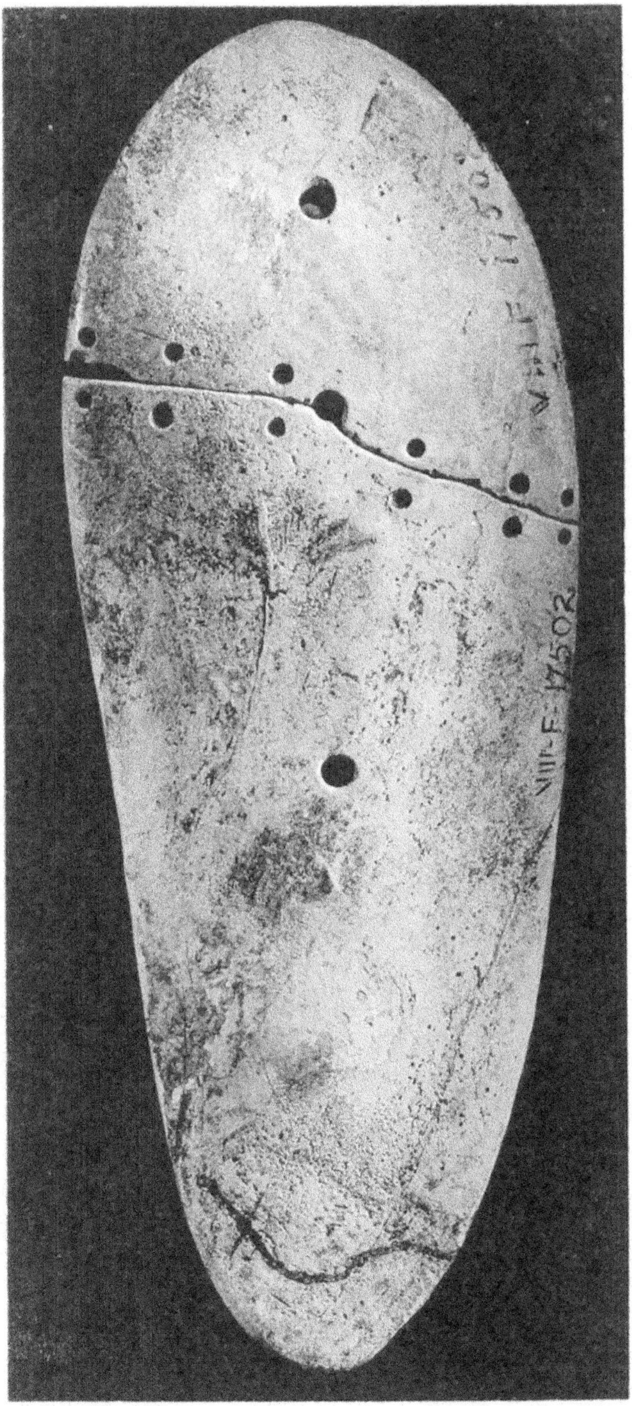

PLATE VI

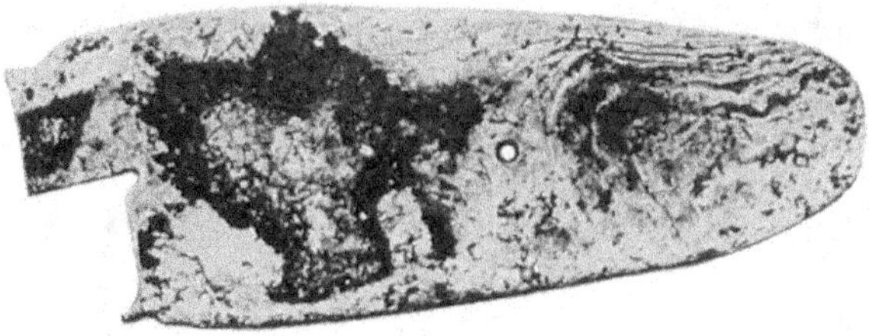

Fig. 1

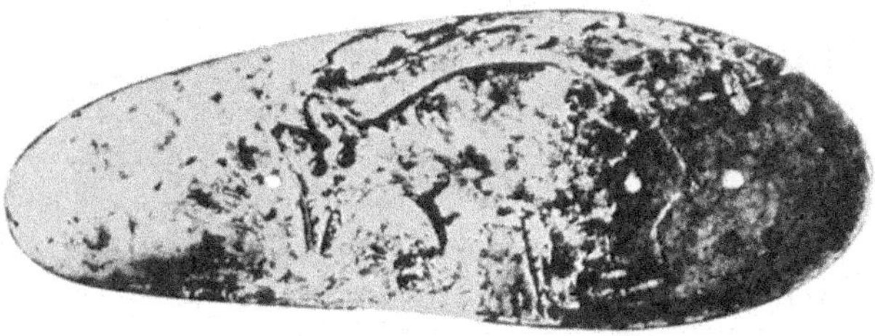

Fig. 2

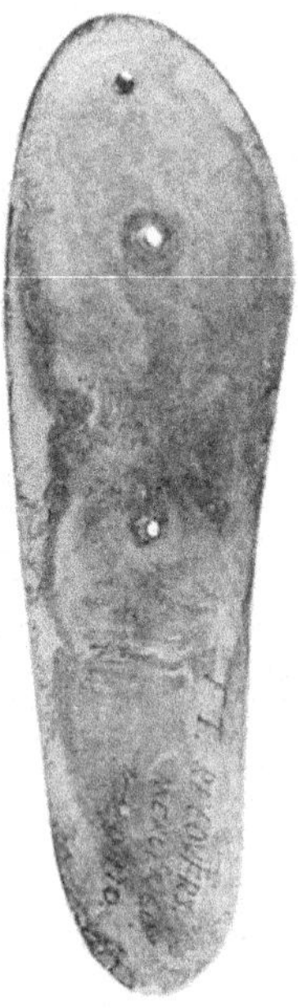

Fig. 3

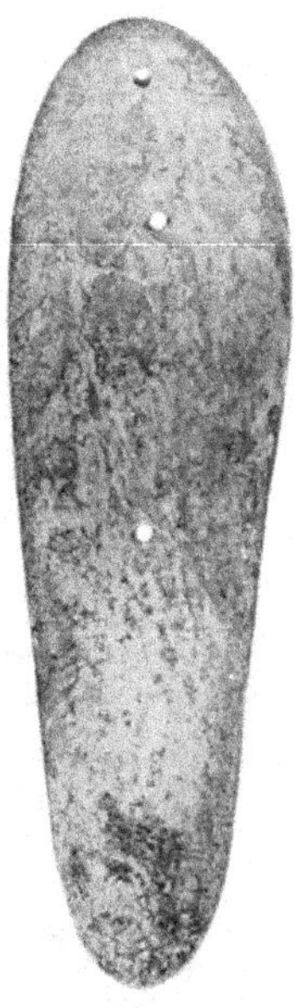

Fig. 4

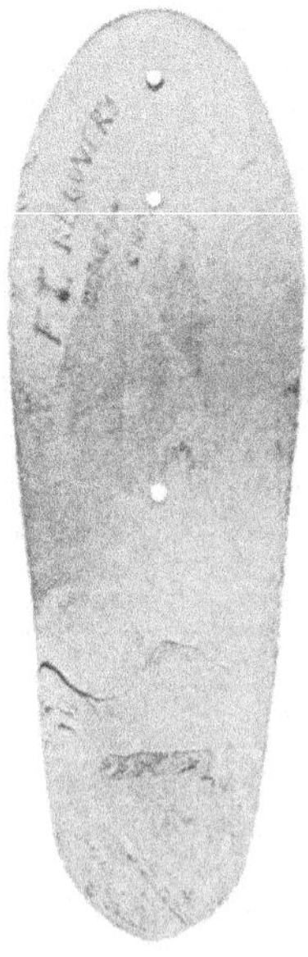

Fig. 5

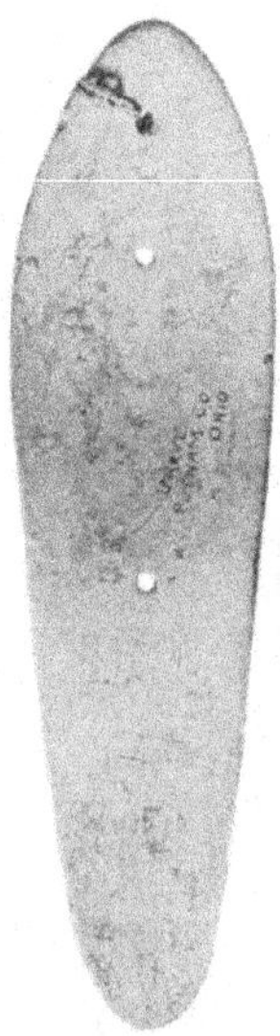

Fig. 6

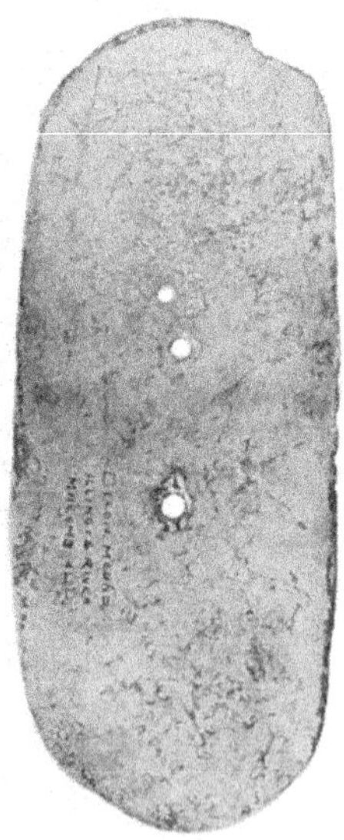

Fig. 7

PLATE VI

Fig. 1. Broken sandal-sole gorget found with a burial in a gravel bank on the Otis Stiner farm, two miles north of Kenton, Ohio. Ohio State Museum 188/4.

Fig. 2. Engraved sandal-sole gorget from Hardin County, Ohio, with "toe" end restored. Ohio State Museum 190/3.

Figs. 3 and 5. Sandal-sole gorgets from Fort Recovery, Mercer County, Ohio.

Fig. 4. Sandal-sole gorget identified as from "Kahokia Mound," Illinois.

Fig. 6. Sandal-sole gorget from a grave in Putnam County, Ohio.

Fig. 7. Gorget suggestive of the sandal-sole type, probably from a mound in Schuyler County, Illinois.

Figures 3–7 are in the collection of Richard Meyer, of Peoria, Illinois.

PLATE VII

Artifacts from the Mulen site, Randolph County, Indiana, in the Ohio State Museum Collection.

FIG. 1. Engraved sandal-sole gorget.

FIG. 2. Sandal-sole gorget.

FIG. 3. Broken sandal-sole gorget marked with incised lines forming cross-hatched bands.

FIG. 4. Celt of black slate.

FIG. 5. Tubular pipe of limestone.

PLATE VII

Fig. 1

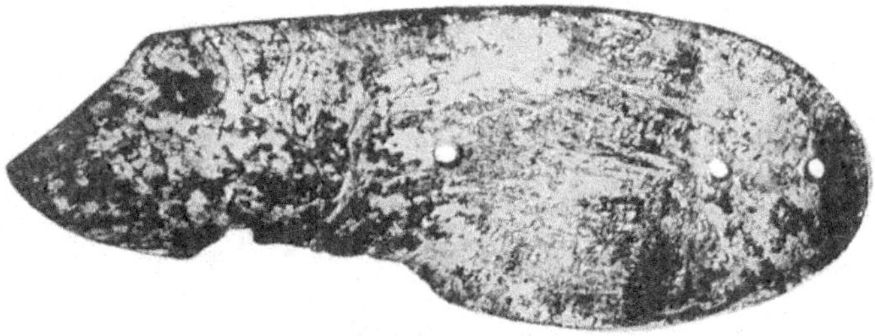

Fig. 2

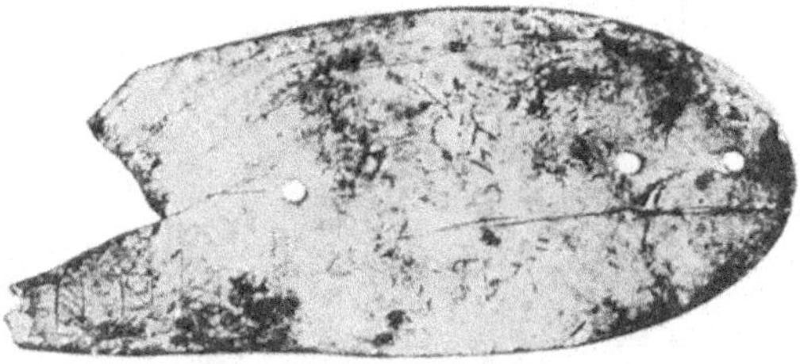

Fig. 3

Fig. 4

Fig. 5

PLATE VIII

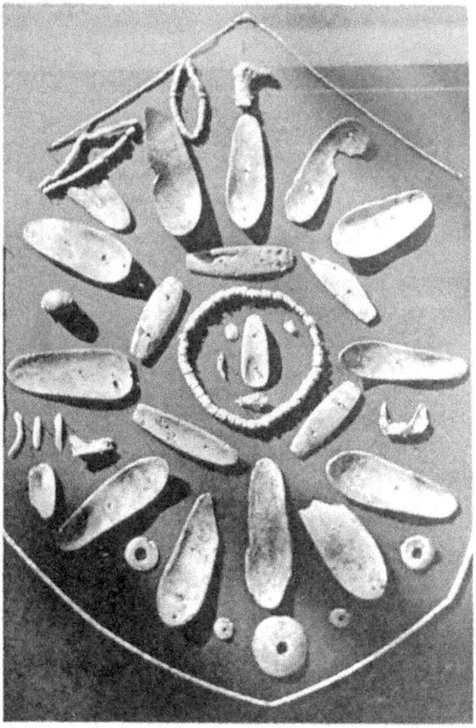

Fig. 1

Fig. 2

PLATE VIII

FIG. 1. Shell and bone artifacts from the Zimmerman site, Hardin County, Ohio.

FIG. 2. A marine gastropod (*Cassis* sp.?) shell, a small string of copper beads, a large string of copper beads, and a small Woodland vessel from the Zimmerman site.

PLATE IX

Shell gorgets from the Ridgeway site, Mercer County, Ohio. Reproduced from the *Ohio Centennial Report.*

PLATE IX

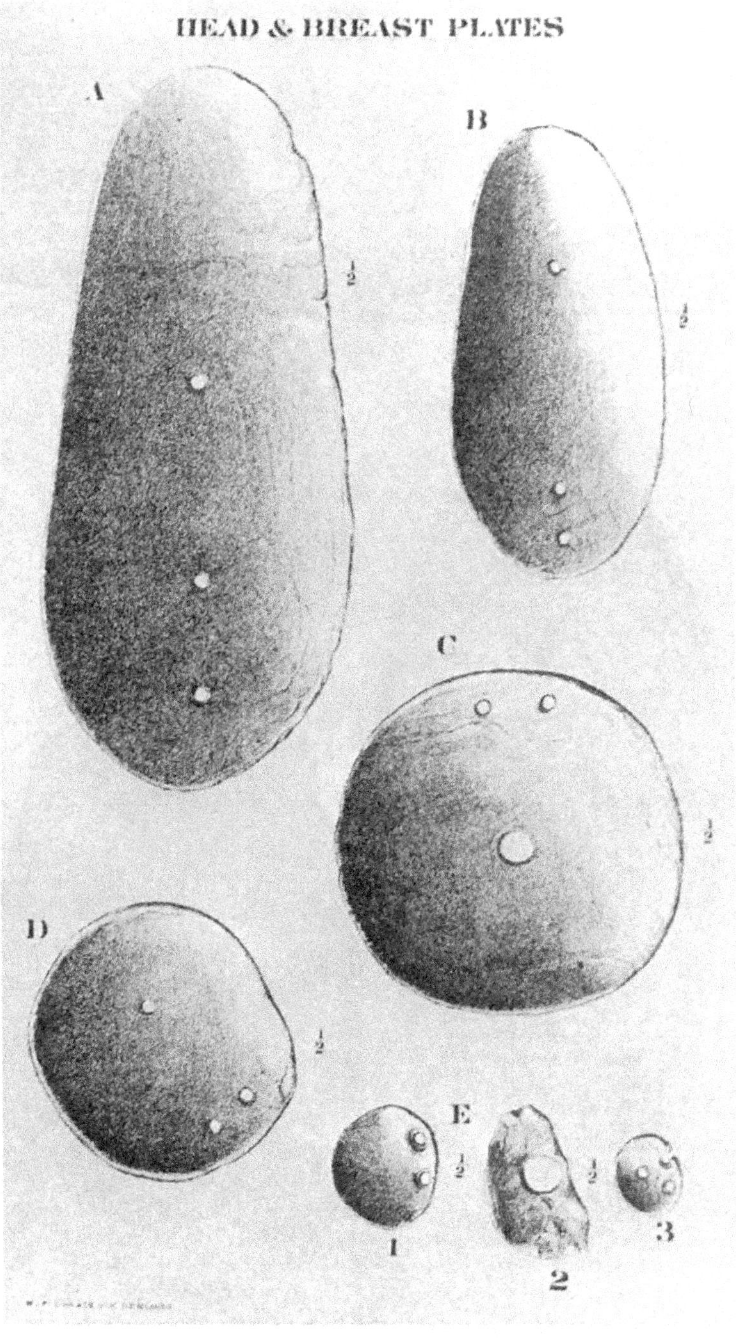

PLATE X

FIG. 1

FIG. 2

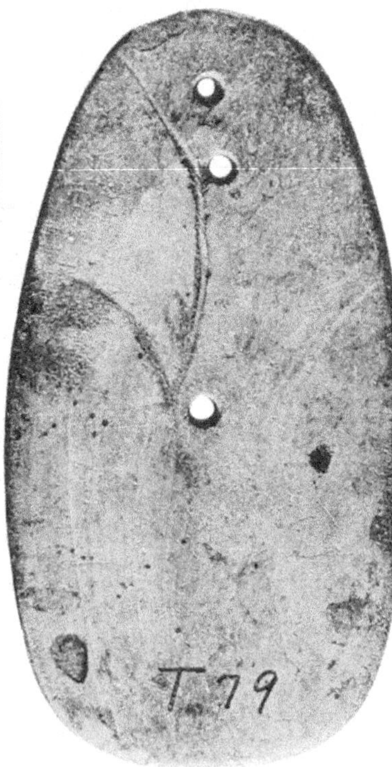

FIG. 3

PLATE X

FIG. 1. Large, flat-base platform pipe, probably of red Ohio pipestone. This pipe was with a skeleton in a gravel pit in Allen County, Indiana, at a depth of ten feet. Two sandal-sole gorgets and a circular disk gorget with one perforation were also with the burial. The pipe is eight and one-half inches long, and the stem end is at the left. Photograph by courtesy of the Museum of the American Indian, Heye Foundation.

FIG. 2. Slate gorget found on the surface in Van Buren County, Michigan.

FIG. 3. Slate gorget found on the surface in Berrien County, Michigan. The gorgets are reproduced from a photograph by Richard M. Snodgrasse.

PLATE XI

FIG. 1. Front view of a skull, with the lower jaw missing, from the Burch site, near Coldwater, Branch County, Michigan.

FIG. 2. Side view of skull from the Burch site.

Photographs by Richard M. Snodgrasse.

PLATE XI

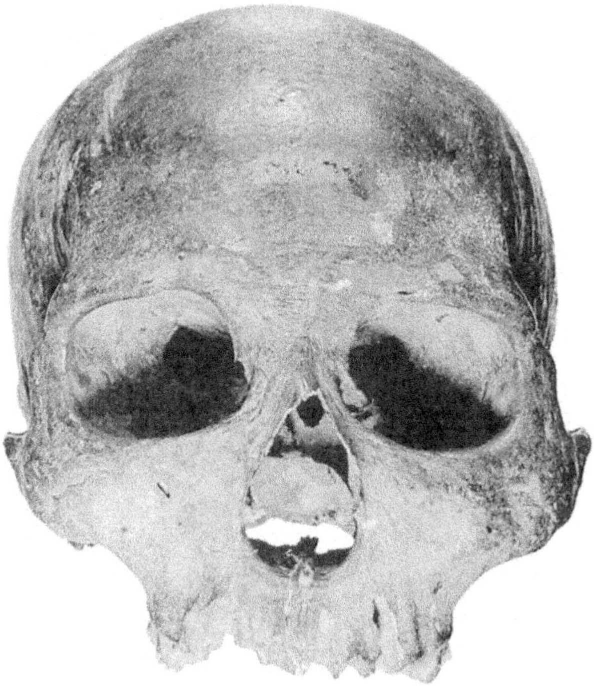

FIG. 1

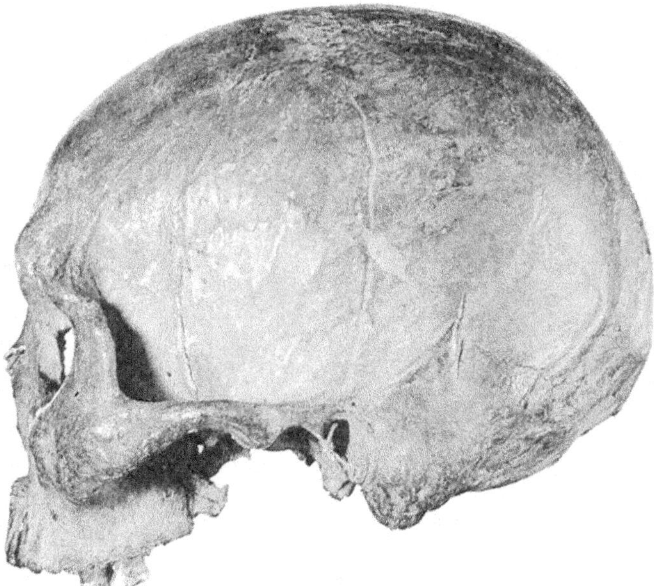

FIG. 2

www.ingramcontent.com/pod-product-compliance
Lightning Source LLC
LaVergne TN
LVHW050022250826
846302LV00008B/62
* 9 7 8 1 9 4 9 0 9 8 5 2 5 *